Contents

This book is dedicated to the real Sue, Felicia, Mary, Tommy, Freda, Sally, Dave, Fran, Faye, Olga, Carmen, Max, Scott, Kyle, Sonja, Tray, and Connie, whose friendships I will always treasure. And to all the other peer counselors in my classes who inspired, encouraged, and motivated me.

And it is dedicated to my husband, Roy, and our eight children: Alissa, David, Matthew, Kimberly, Paul, Timothy, John, and Elizabeth, whose love and understanding have been a constant support.

Acknowledgments

From the conception of this book to the finish, many people have contributed to its becoming a reality.

I would like to thank Dana Leigh Taylor, a TV writer who visited my class and was one of the first to encourage me to write this book.

To Delle Chatman, the TV writer working on a Walt Disney project with our peer counselors who had faith in my ability to write this book alone, although she agreed to help write it if I found it to be an impossible task. Thank you, Delle, for assuring me I could solo on my first flight.

To Carl and Becky Walter, friends of many years, who were the first readers of the beginning chapter and who said, "You can do it."

To all the peer counselors who spent hours of their busy time in my living room, reading, suggesting, correcting, and encouraging. And to Valerie Gibson, in particular, who has continued to support my efforts on a regular basis.

To new friends I have met because of writing this book. To Dr. Marion Pollock—a real wordsmith—who taught me many lessons about word usage. Dr. Pollock, I promise never to use the word "hopefully."

To Sarah Edwards whose expertise, belief in peer counseling and understanding of teenagers made her the perfect editor. Her warm, friendly personality, tenacity for details, and willingness to work long and hard in order to achieve the best possible results made working with her a delight. A very special thanks, Sarah, for working with a new writer—and not making me feel like one.

To the friends who read the manuscript and endorsed my book: Dr. Michael Durfee, Susan Newman, Dr. Barbara Varenhorst, Robert W. Gibson, Dr. Marion Pollock, Dr. Irving Berkovitz. Your support is appreciated immensely.

To two good friends of peer counseling, Jaye Moseley, who added much to our work and whose humanity makes this world a better place, and to Dr. Stuart Gothold, whose support of our program was always outstanding.

To Ben Lizardi whose design expertise has turned my manuscript into a beautiful book.

To my husband and family who have been understanding of the many hours that I've been at the computer—who, in spite of their own inconveniences, have encouraged me to "stay with it."

And, finally to the men and women whose work produced the wonderful machine that has become my friend, my Macintosh computer. In spite of frustrations at times with problems, such as "It" losing one of my chapters, I really wouldn't have wanted to write the book without it.

To all of you listed above—and many other friends who helped —I say most sincerely, THANK YOU.

—Joan Sturkie

Foreword

Peer counseling has inspired me. The ability for students to nurture, protect, educate, and to value each other offers reassurance that the world will survive humanity's propensity toward destruction.

Student peer groups are a real and valuable resource to the many "war-against" programs the adult world has launched. A peer group can become a powerful deterrent to self destructive behaviors. Drug and alcohol abuse, sexual promiscuity and teen pregnancy, social isolation, depression and suicide, and general school and social failure all become issues for the peer group to address.

Students learn to handle problems with others more thoughtfully. New students are greeted rather than ignored, tested, or ostracized. Teachers come to be viewed as people worthy of respect. Family problems are seen from reasonable perspectives. Even crises as severe as child molestation, rape and the death of a friend become more manageable with the support of others.

Words like respect, responsibility, concern, and even love take on new meaning. More than anything, the peer counselors learn to apply these words first to themselves and then to others.

The realities of life and the limitation of school resources call for the expansion of peer counseling to all campuses.The basic requirement for this program to take root and flourish in a school is simple. The adults involved must believe in the viability of having students serve as a valued resource. They must believe in the students and hold their efforts in high regard.

While there are lessons to learn about psychology and counseling techniques, the basic lesson for the students is to believe in themselves and their innate ability to be of value to others. Peer counseling is not for a narrow group of student leaders. It is an opportunity for human beings, who happen to be students, to learn how to more thoughtfully care for themselves and others.

I was not always an advocate for a structured peer counseling format. Initially I told the author of this book that the program would not work. I did not appreciate the incredible ability of students to reach out to each other so powerfully. The students have taught us all.

Students are a resource.They can be a damaging influence on each other's lives or become a powerful force for thoughtful action. Peer counseling creates a platform for the latter. It provides a foundation for constructive behavior both in school and later throughout their lives. The saying goes, ''ONCE A PEER COUNSELOR, ALWAYS A PEER COUNSELOR.'' I believe in that phase and in this program.

Dr. Michael Durfee, M.D
Child Psychiatrist
Coordinator of Child Abuse Prevention Program,
Los Angeles County Department of Health Service.
Assistant Clinical Professor in Psychiatry and Pediatrics,
University of Southern California, School of Medicine

PART I

Introduction

''When I entered this class I felt like garbage. Now I feel like a worthwhile human being.''

''Our class is like a family. We trust and care about each other.''

''I've learned to help other people, but I've also learned how to help myself.''

These are comments from high school students talking about a very special class I taught for three years. A unique class, but one similar also to traditional classes. Not all schools offer it, so you may or may not know about it. The class is called peer counseling.

I wrote this book because I wanted you to see what I saw, hear what I heard, and grow in understanding as I grew. I experienced new insights, compassion, and tolerance because every day I had the privilege of sitting in a circle with a group of wonderful, energetic, happy teenagers—who also were sometimes hurting, fearful, depressed. Again, I was able to reaffirm my basic belief that young people are one of our most valued resources. As well-intending as we may be, too often as adults we want to "help" solve the teenagers' problems by imposing our solutions and remedies on them. I believe that it is time that we train these kids to help each other, allow them to use all their abundant energy and basic peer knowledge, and stand by, available to them as they demonstrate their abilities. I have written this book because these young people have already proven what they can do, and by reading their stories you will be able to see how capable and resourceful they are.

For many adults, the word "teenager" brings negative adjectives to mind. With hope, this book will replace some of those negative thoughts with positive ones.

This book is written for three different groups of people:

- For teenagers themselves—To help young people see that they are not alone. Other teenagers have had similar problems and have learned how to resolve them.

- For parents, grandparents, aunts, uncles, and other relatives—To allow them to see the teen problems they fear through the eyes of the young people and gain new insights and solutions.

- For teachers, counselors, administrators, and school board members—To allow them to see what a positive impact having a peer counseling program on their high school campus can have on the lives of their students.

As you read this book, you will find that it is actually a series of stories about real life events. You will meet and come to know many of the students. You will live through the experiences they faced and struggle with them in finding solutions. The names of all the characters in this book have been changed to protect confidentiality, but they are all real people who lived through these real events. The students have given me written permission to tell their stories. Their desire is to continue to help their peers, whether it be by personal contact or through the written page.

When you finish reading this, you may want to be part of a peer counseling program, so I have closed the book with my suggestions for how you can start a program like this in your school.

Now before you begin to relive my journey of the past few years, I would like to provide you with some background about peer counseling.

What is peer counseling?

Peer counseling is a program where adolescents learn how to correctly and positively support one another.

A peer counselor is a person who cares about others and takes time to listen to their problems. Without giving advice, the peer counselor assists the person in solving his or her own problems. By using active listening and counseling skills, the young person helps counselees clarify their feelings and look for the available solutions.

One student defined peer counseling as, "A class composed of trained, caring people who are willing to extend themselves to help others."

In their book, *Peer Counseling: Skills and Perspectives,* Dr. Vincent D'Andrea and Peter Salovey define it as, "The use of active listening and problem-solving skills, along with knowledge about human growth and mental health, to counsel people who are our peers—peers in age, status, and knowledge.''

Los Angeles County Superintendent of Schools Dr. Stuart Gothold writes in a Los Angeles PTA Bulletin, ''I think there is a message offered by peer counseling. The message is that as the world gets increasingly complicated—which it will—adults may become less and less equipped to deal with the complex feelings of young people as they grow up. Peer counseling suggests that in some cases it may be a good idea for adults to admit they are overwhelmed, not feel guilty about it, and find other ways of helping. In this case—and in many others—that help could come in the form of helping kids help other kids. After all, they do speak the same language.''

Peers helping peers is not a new concept. As far back as Biblical times the author of Ecclesiastes wrote, ''Two are better than one. For if they fall, the one will lift up his fellow; but woe to him that is alone when he falleth; for he hath not another to help him up.''

Children have been taught and encouraged to function as instructional agents for their classroom peers since the early 1800's. However, it was not until the late 1960's that peer counseling was studied in a rigorous fashion. Since that time, it has been used with increasing acceptance and success. With student problems being spotlighted during the 1980's, and the demands on high school counselors' time increasing, peer counseling has spread to schools throughout the country.

Students are learning how to help each other through systematic training. This training may be delivered differently, but ideally the outcome is the same—that students are trained and effective in helping their peers resolve problems.

The format used varies from school to school. Some schools offer peer counseling as a course that meets on a daily basis during the normal school day. The same amount of credit is earned in this class as in any other class on campus.The students develop the skills the first semester, and use them in their role as peer counselors on campus during following semesters. They continue to meet daily in their advanced peer counseling classes for as many semesters as the school allows or as long as they wish to remain in the program.

Other schools offer the class before or after school or during the summer for a given number of weeks. After the training is completed the peer counselors continue to meet at a scheduled time—usually bi-weekly or weekly. Members of this class may or may not receive high school credits.

In top universities, data from scientific studies are being compiled to verify how effective peer counselors are. A recent study conducted by Dr. S.B. Kar, John Talbot and Carl Coan assessed the effectiveness of teen peer counselors in the prevention of unwanted teen pregnancies and compared their performance with that of adult professionals. The summary of that study was, "We conclude that peer counselors can perform an extremely valuable function as an adjunct to the clinical services provided by the professionals; and, in do ing so, they can significantly enhance the overall efficiency of various family planning programmes designed to serve teens—."

I have written this book based on my experience with peer counselors on a high school campus.The guidelines and activities I described, however, may be used in any peer counseling situation. Peer counseling is not limited to the school system. It is used successfully in senior citizen facilities, in Planned Parenthood Clinics, in drug abuse half-way homes, in police academies—the list is endless.

My hope is that by reading this book, you will be inspired and enriched by these teenagers who relate their stories—and in so being, you will reach out to the young people around you. John Steinbeck wrote, "I have had many teachers who told me soon-forgotten facts but only three who created in me a new attitude and a new hunger." May you—whether you be a classroom teacher, a counselor, a mother, father, grandparent, aunt, uncle, friend, or fellow student—be one of those three.

PART II

CHAPTER ONE

Love— The Secret Ingredient

The teddy bear's eyes seemed to say ''please don't leave me here alone,'' but I slammed shut the metal door and closed the symbol of so many memories into the darkness of the cabinet. I had a job to do and I must do it.

Crossing the room, I opened the upper drawer of the four-drawer file and began purging it of out-of-date reports and personal memorabilia. I wanted everything to be in order for the next peer counseling teacher, so he or she wouldn't have any trouble finding the supplemental material I had collected. Two large trash cans sat waiting beside me, and as I stuffed them with papers, I wondered why I hadn't cleaned out this file earlier in the school year. I would've enjoyed being able to put my hands immediately on any newspaper clippings, magazine articles, or personal notes that related to my subject matter.

At last, only the bottom drawer—the catch-all—was left

to comb meticulously. I reached to the back, sorted through a stack of papers piled on the bottom, and found a blue loose-leaf notebook with "Joel" written almost illegibly on the cover. I picked the notebook up and flipped it open. Inside were weekly entries in a journal meant to be read only by the teacher and student.

I'd never liked keeping these notebooks longer than overnight because what was in them was confidential and very personal. But Joel had left school suddenly, and I hadn't had a chance to return it. Besides, I'd kept hoping he'd come back for a visit. Sacramento was only a few hundred miles away and peer counselors had a habit of returning "home" to sit in the familiar circle and share their experiences. Joel hadn't come back though. He was with his father, who Joel's mother had described as, "a strong man who can straighten this kid out."

I looked up from the book, remembering how those words had rung in my ears the day Joel's mother sat in my counseling office. This expensively-dressed executive had come to check her son out of school. But she couldn't be talking about the same boy I knew. Joel had been shy, and because he had entered the peer counseling class a month late, he sat for weeks before he trusted his fellow students enough to share the feelings of loneliness and rejection he'd held inside so long.

I remembered his history. Joel's parents were divorced. He lived with his father until his father remarried a woman in her early twenties. The young bride didn't want a 16 year old son living in her new home, so Joel was told it "would be best for him" to live with his mother in Southern California.

Joel had never gotten along with his mother because he

felt she didn't want him and looked on him as an inconvenience to her career in the highly-competitive world of fashion. But his father, too, was living in the fast lane. He was promoting a career as a government lobbyist, and this seemed incompatible with solving his drinking problem. The late-night meetings he attended usually ended up with his entertaining important people at the bar, where temptation yanked him off the wagon he was trying to ride. Joel spoke of his father as a "great guy when he was sober," but as a verbally abusive, unreasonable man when he was drunk.

The notebook, which I was still holding, contained the feelings of a 16 year old boy trying to find his identity in a world where his parents were trying to do the same, each with apparently little support. But whether Joel was in Sacramento with his father or in Southern California with his mother, he had felt unwanted and unloved.

So what should I do? I couldn't throw that notebook into the trash because it was a testimony to a time in Joel's life when he had found love, acceptance, and respect from a group of 35 high school students. Those students had helped this new boy at school feel as though he belonged, and his writings told how good that felt. Maybe sometime Joel would need to read about that period in his life and thus assure himself that he could trust and share his feelings with another group. I hoped so, and put the notebook in the box of personal items I was going to take home. Maybe Joel would come back to visit his mother sometime and call me.

With the desk cleaned out, the metal cabinet straightened, and now the four-drawer file in order, I was free to leave the room that held so many memories for me. I looked around. High ceilings, carpeted floor, walls without windows, but inside were the various trappings of a student activity center. Then there were the murals—walls filled with vivid colors, painted by students to portray their dreams, their world-awareness. I walked toward the door, the box of personal belongings in hand, remembering how perfect this room had been for a peer counseling class. There were no conventional-style desks, only armless chairs which were placed in a circle that could be made smaller if a number of students were away on a field trip or larger if alumni returned or other visitors joined us, like administrators from other schools, TV writers, or students with a problem. A large room need not seem cold and impersonal, I thought, if a group of people with caring spirits and concern for others enters its walls. And people like that had certainly been in here. . . .

Suddenly I knew I couldn't leave. Not yet anyway. I had to say good-bye to all the loving spirits, the energy I could feel around me.

I put my box on one of the chairs and sat down beside it, hardly able to believe that three years had gone by since I entered this room to teach the first peer counseling class our high school ever had. At that time, I'd been a counselor at the school for six years and had learned that no matter how hard I worked, I couldn't hope to meet the needs of 350 students. I'd also learned that our school, with 1050, was lucky to have even three counselors. Many schools had fewer counselors and more students.

The personal counseling needs of students seemed to be growing while at the same time there were more expectations for the counselor to address other issues, such as academic, college, and career counseling. We needed more time than the 10 to12 hour day that we were already spending at school and more ears to listen to the multitude of student problems.

I had the idea for a peer counseling class at our high school in 1980 when a student told me of the feelings of loneliness, fright, and depression she experienced before and after an abortion. Before she left my counseling office that day she said, "I would be glad to talk to any student who might find herself in the same situation I've just gone through. I wish I'd had a friend to relate to when times were so bad for me."

It was then I realized, if we could train students in counseling skills and supervise them in a controlled environment, then the adult counselors would, as it were, have "extended hands" and therefore could reach more students. Adults have always known that teenagers spend much of their time talking to each other—the many hours they spend on the telephone is a good example of this. If they could be taught active listening skills, body language, "I" messages, community resource referrals, all of these things and more, then they could help each other. They could alert counselors or teachers to serious problems that might otherwise go undetected. And, in so doing, they would also acquire coping skills that would equip them to be better prepared for life.

With this in mind, I started my two year quest to get a peer counseling course in our curriculum. This dream became a reality when a Title IVC grant from the state of California for peer counseling was awarded to our school. The first class was open only to juniors and seniors, and 25 students were chosen from a sign-up list of 60 students. Personal interviews by two counselors, with each interviewing the candidates separately, were held so that the class would reflect a representation of each ethnic group, social group (Socies, Preppies, Heavy Metalers, Punkers), academic and attendance groups, and a general cross-section of the school campus.

From that beginning class the first semester, the program began to grow. The second semester there were two classes: one beginning class where skills were taught and practiced and one advanced class where the students were still practicing their skills in class, growing as individuals, and actually going out and being peer counselors on campus.

The third semester there were three classes. When the need for four sections was apparent, I realized that another teacher would need to be trained. I was carrying a full counseling load, and teaching three classes at that time. Fortunately, a social science teacher was interested in the program, and he agreed to take the fourth section. At the beginning of the sixth semester, a need for a fifth section was evident. At that time, an English teacher expressed an interest, and she taught a beginning class. During that sixth semester of peer counseling, I taught three advanced classes, the social studies teacher taught an advanced class, and the English teacher taught a beginning class. A total of 150 students were enrolled in five classes. It had become the elective most in demand by students.

What was the secret ingredient of this popular class? Why would students with poor attendance in other classes always show up for this class? What made students visit the class after graduation and be concerned about their friends who were still underclassmen on campus?

The secret ingredient was LOVE.

The love and respect from one student to another; the concern, respect, and love for the students by the teachers; the acceptance of each race for the other; the understanding by the popular student of the peer who had not participated in any phase of school activities; the patience and understanding for the handicapped student; the reaching out to the student who had lost his best friend in a car accident or whose father had succumbed to a heart attack; the concern and commitment to encourage the classmate who had achieved 45 days of sobriety—these were the things that set this class apart from other classes.

This class was different. Students not only learned in the traditional way, but they learned from interacting with each other: listening, encouraging, helping, experiencing, loving.

Peer counseling teachers and students from other schools often visited our classroom to observe, and the most frequent comment that I heard from the visitors was, "You teach the same material I teach, but your class is different. One can feel the love in this room." The next question would always be, "How do I put these feelings into my classroom?" The person actually was asking, "Can love be taught?"

I don't believe you teach love. You give love—and when love is given, the giver acquires a greater capacity to love. That's how it worked in our class. But before one can give love, one must first learn to love himself. An example of this was Tommy.

Tommy came to class looking like one of those children you see in magazine ads asking for donations to feed the hungry. He appeared to weigh less than one hundred pounds, and even though he was small in stature, I felt that a well-balanced diet would do wonders for this shy, withdrawn boy. His hollow eyes seemed never to make contact with the eyes of other students. I had the feeling that he was afraid to allow others to look in his eyes for fear they would see beyond the pupils into the hurt and pain his 15 years had brought. His tattered jeans and faded shirt, together with his uncombed blond hair and sad face, gave him the appearance of being a person other students would not seek out as a friend. Because the students were never assigned seats (quite the contrary, they were encouraged to sit next to a different person each day), I was amazed to see Mollie come into the room day by day and sit in the vacant seat next to Tommy.

When Tommy was absent two days in a row, Mollie stayed after class to tell me that she had called Tommy the night before—the students always shared their phone numbers with everyone in class. Mollie had learned that Tommy's father was away for five days on a cross-country trucking job, and now Tommy was alone at home with the flu. Tommy had been told by his father that should an emergency arise while he was out of town, Tommy could call his aunt who lived several miles away. But Tommy was not inclined to seek help from his aunt. She was an impatient, overworked mother of six who found the burden of raising children alone, plus having to work two jobs to support them, almost too much to bear. Tommy didn't feel that he wanted to add one more responsibility to her already joyless existence.

Mollie shared with me that she had decided weeks ago, when Tommy first entered the class, to commit herself to be his friend and to achieve one goal before her graduation in June. This 18 year old girl's goal was to see that Tommy felt accepted in this class, and that his self-esteem would grow to a point that it was evident to others—and especially to Tommy himself.

When Tommy returned to school, he was welcomed not only by Mollie, but by the entire class. Words to the effect of, "Hey, man, we missed you," "Glad you're back," "How are you feeling?" were heard as the students found seats before the tardy bell. One could tell that so much attention made Tommy feel somewhat uncomfortable. His eyes were still downcast, with only a glance now and then in the direction of those who were speaking. But his inhibited responses did not deter the group from showing Tommy they cared about him.

Mollie had succeeded in getting the class involved in her project, and now others in the group were making a special effort to sit next to Tommy and spend a few moments engaging in conversation with him before and after class. Whenever Tommy was absent, Mollie saw to it that at least three people in the class called to tell him he was missed. And that was the truth, because by this time Tommy was missed whenever he wasn't there. Even though his verbal contribution to the class was limited, his uniqueness was a part of the class; and when that uniqueness was gone, a part of the class was missing.

When students worked in groups, Tommy was immediately included. He was encouraged to express his ideas, but pressure was never applied. The students were very sensitive to the fact that "Rome was not built in a day" and neither was Tommy's behavior to change immediately. He was praised when he contributed, and over the months the group learned that Tommy could share some of the most profound and stimulating insights. He was listened to, respected, and included, just like any other student in class.

One day, Greg, the 165-pound star of the varsity wrestling team, expressed concern about his team's lack of preparation for the new season. The team still needed an athlete who could compete in the 101-pound category. One boy the team had counted on was out for the season with a broken leg from a skiing accident. To forfeit this weight category at each match would certainly leave the team in trouble for tournaments and league play-offs.

Mollie, using her quick intelligence, turned to Tommy and asked him how much he weighed. The days of being teased and called a shrimp, a weakling, or a small-fry immediately reflected on Tommy's face. The tension in class mounted as all eyes glanced to Mollie as if to ask, "How could you do that to Tommy?"

"Nearly a hundred," Tommy murmured under his breath, with his eyes cast down to the floor.

At this point, Greg, obviously more concerned with Tommy's feelings than the plight of the wrestling team, jumped in with, "Would you be interested in trying out for the wrestling team?"

As could be expected, Tommy stated in no uncertain terms that he would not. His diminutive build had convinced him long ago that he could never be an athlete. Even when he was younger and his classmates in elementary school were playing Little League baseball, Tommy did not participate. He had wanted to, but his father was not available on Saturdays to sign him up and to pay the fee.

Later, when Tommy heard the other boys talking about their Moms and Dads being at every game, he was glad that he wasn't on the team. At least, no one would ask why his parents were not there. He really didn't want to think up stories that were untrue, and he certainly wasn't going to tell them that he hadn't seen his mother since he was two years old and wouldn't even recognize her if she did show up at a game. And he knew from past experiences that his father would never attend a game. Somehow he managed to be out of town on some long trucking haul at just those times Tommy most wanted him home, like on his birthday.

So "NO," Tommy certainly did not want to be on the wrestling team. But after the initial shock of trying to protect Tommy from what he perceived as an unfortunate remark, Greg began to toy with the possibility that Tommy might actually be able to build up some muscle and learn the wrestling moves well enough to participate in the first match of the season. After all, Tommy was intelligent, and being able to think quickly, as well as to move quickly, was certainly an asset for a wrestler. Wrestling was a sport that did not discriminate against lightweights, but made room for them; in fact, needed them.

The class never knew just how Tommy was persuaded to try out for the team. We all relied on Greg's good judgment and believed that he would work effectively without using pressure. I heard that Greg invited Tommy to several of the practices "just to watch."

After a few weeks, Greg and Tommy became inseparable.

With the school requiring a "C" average for students participating in school athletics, Tommy had to dust the cobwebs off his books and wake up that part of his brain he had left slumbering for years. Greg tutored him each night, always scheduling their lessons around meal time at Greg's house. There, his warm and affectionate, size 14½ mother was delighted to have an extra guest to share the bounty of food she so lovingly supplied her husband and three sons. Soon, it was apparent that with the new nourishment he was receiving, only long hours of work-outs in the gym would keep Tommy's weight from exceeding 101 pounds. He was quickly developing brawn. The improved diet was replacing his old pallor with a healthy glow. That haunting, gaunt look was gone forever. And as the weeks passed, Tommy continued to flourish.

When the wrestling season came to an end, the entire peer counseling class attended the league championships. Greg placed first in his category, qualifying him to go on toward the state competitions which meant so much to him in this, his senior year. Tommy placed fourth in the 101-weight category, not qualifying him to advance, but he had two more years in high school to work toward that goal. And we all knew he would reach it, because we had witnessed the evolution of a new Tommy. We had seen him become a determined, confident young man who was proud of his size and eager to find ways of capitalizing on it.

The last day of class before graduation, a feeling of sadness seemed to permeate the room. At least a third of the class were seniors, and this would be the last time they would all be together. Oh, some would return to visit, but others, like the two foreign exchange students, might never return. These 35 students would probably never all be together in this room again. Never again would the many be made one. Never this precise synthesis of young humanity that had laughed and cried in unison. So much had happened to each of them. They had entered the class in many different ways—some as friends, some as strangers, others as slight acquaintances—but they were all leaving as friends, and more. As one student expressed it, ''We're more than just good friends now. We're a family.''

After they finished the final examination, a spontaneous cry rose up from the group, all at the same time:

''Let's do the teddy bear!''

''Doing the teddy bear'' was the most popular activity in the class and was saved for one or two special times during each semester. This activity had been introduced to the very first peer counseling class three years ago by a visiting college student from San Diego. He was the boyfriend of a classmate's sister. I hope someday, that young man learns what an impact his one visit made on all the future peer counseling classes at our school.

"Doing the teddy bear" meant sitting in a circle and giving this soft stuffed animal to a person toward whom you especially wanted to show love or appreciation, or to a person for whom you had a special message. I always started the teddy bear on his way, selecting a student who I felt had shown great improvement or had accomplished something in another aspect of school, or someone who was experiencing a very difficult time in his or her life. The person presenting the teddy bear never mentioned the name of the intended recipient until the very end of his comments.

I gave the bear to one of the foreign exchange students saying, "I want this teddy bear to go to a student who has added so very much to this class by always having a smile for everyone. This person has been very willing to help fellow students in and out of this class. She has been an exemplary peer counselor, acquiring skills that she'll use for the rest of her life. I personally will miss this student very much because her caring, unselfish personality has enriched my life. I want to give this to Eva."

I rose from my chair and took the teddy to Eva. I gave her a hug with the teddy bear. Then she chose someone else in the room to praise and love, and presented that person with the bear.

This would continue until each person had received the teddy bear. Some would receive it several times. The rule was that each comment had to be completely honest, and, since one person might want to give it to someone who had already received it, we always allowed that to happen.

Rita, the energetic, sophomore cheerleader said, "I want to give this to someone that I am so proud of. I have seen this person achieve academically, athletically, and socially. He was a total stranger to me a few months ago, and honestly, I would never have gotten to know him if he hadn't been in this class. When he first entered the class, I thought he was a loner, and wanted to remain that way. Being such a extrovert myself, I really couldn't relate to him at all. I just want to say "thank you" to this person for allowing me to feel that I now understand and accept people who have different personalities than mine. I now know that we each have something important to give to one another. I want to give this teddy bear to a person who has become very special to me. I want to give it to Tommy."

As she walked toward his chair, Tommy jumped up and met her in center circle, sweeping the petite, sophomore girl up in a bear hug that lifted her off the floor. His wrestling muscles were still in good shape. The entire class broke out in applause, and the box of tissues was quickly circulated around the room. I glanced at Mollie, and her face shone with the satisfaction of one who had achieved a very challenging and worthwhile goal. No one in the room other than Mollie and I knew about that goal. Our eyes met in an all-knowing glance and a smile crossed both of our faces. I knew that this was a moment Mollie would never forget, nor would I.

Tommy sat back down and hugged the teddy bear close to his chest. He had reached a new maturity that allowed a boy to hug a teddy bear without feeling any less a man. The room was again so silent you could hear a pin drop. For a few seconds, Tommy did not say a word. He just sat there with his eyes looking down at the floor and his arms clutching the bear. I had the feeling he was replaying in his mind the events of the last year. When he lifted his head, a solemn, almost painful expression was on his face.

''I want to give this teddy bear to a person who—.'' His words seemed to fade, and he hesitated before he continued. After a brief pause, new strength appeared, and he continued in a strong voice, ''Knowing this person has changed my life. When I first came into this class, I felt like garbage. Now I feel like a human being. This person, along with this class, has shown me that I can make something of my life. I don't have to just let things happen to me because of circumstances. I can take charge of my life.''

For a once shy boy who only spoke in three to five-word sentences, this speech was a monumental undertaking. The air was so emotionally charged at this point that I could see tears in the eyes of both the boys and the girls in the circle. He continued, ''I just want to say to this person, 'Thank you, Greg. Thank you for everything. I love you like a brother.' ''

Greg had already gotten up, and this time it was Tommy who was lifted from the floor in a bear hug. Greg's 165 pounds carried the day, and a boy who would always be his friend.

The class continued well after the noon bell sounded. There were no finals on this afternoon of graduation practice, and the class didn't want to stop for lunch, which most adults might find difficult to believe. Aren't teenagers always hungry?

Everyone had received the bear more than one time, and I kept it when it was given to me. I reminded the seniors that they, along with me, were due on the field for graduation practice in ten minutes. There were hugs for everyone as we left that final day, and many promises to meet next year for a reunion— "Let's all come no matter where we are."

The bell brought me back from my memories of that graduation week, and I glanced up at the clock to realize that I had been sitting in the room for over a half hour. How strange bells sound when there are no students on campus to hear them. It's a sound of loneliness, like the whistle of a train in the night.

I quickly rose from the chair, as if to visibly shake off the melancholy mood. I started walking the few feet to the door where sunshine, green grass, and blue skies lay just beyond.

But I stopped, and in one abrupt motion, I quickly turned, crossed the room to the metal cabinet, opened the door, and reached down and scooped the teddy bear in my arms. His fur was not as clean or as soft as it was three years previously. He had been held in classes totaling over 650 students during the three year period. Tears had fallen on him, sweaty palms had held him, and tensed fingers had clutched him. He had been patted, hugged, and given the honor to be the one legacy of peer counseling that no one ever forgot. I could still hear the questions from beginning students on the first day of each new semester, "When do we get to do the teddy bear?"

I closed the metal door to the cabinet, walked briskly to the front entrance, gave one more quick look around the room, and walked out of a place where I had learned more than probably any one of the students. I had previously thought that being the mother of eight children had given me insight and wisdom. It had, but all of that experience had been limited in comparison to what I had learned from these peer counselors of the past three years. The diversity of the classes and the openness with which they shared their feelings gave me a depth of understanding of teenagers that I had not received elsewhere.

The sunshine felt warm and comforting as I walked across the campus. With Teddy in my arms, I thought how lucky I was to have had the privilege of sharing all of those special moments with a group of very unique and wonderful teenagers.

But now I had something else to do. I had to share the memories, insights, and skills I had learned in peer counseling with other students, teachers, and parents all over the country. And I would begin by asking my students' permission to tell their stories.

CHAPTER TWO

Drugs—
Kids Helping Kids
Get Clean and Sober

Mary sat in the circle and spoke with all of the poise and confidence of a professional speaker. She knew her subject matter well, and she was certainly relating well to this group of peer counselors. They appeared to be hanging on to every word she said. How ironic, I thought, that this person seemed to be one of our most effective speakers. These students had listened to other guests discuss the effects of drugs. Hearing an expert make a presentation was a frequent occurrence in peer counseling classes, and we'd found that even the best qualified and busiest people were willing to give freely of their time and talents to help young people. However, this was not a recognized expert in the field of drug abuse. She had not written a book, received a doctorate, or established a drug rehabilitation program. Quite the contrary, she was 17 years old, a mid-year graduate from high school, and a friend or acquaintance of the students in this classroom. A year ago, she had sat in the same seats that they are sitting in now. I still remembered. . . .

Mary was a beautiful girl with long, chestnut hair that fell loosely around her face. At times she would take both hands and pull her hair away from a face with almost flawless, classic features, and gather it into a pony-tail. Then momentarily she would release it, and again it would fall mid-way down her back. At times, she seemed somewhat nervous, but her upbeat, friendly personality made her such a delight to be around that no one seemed to pay much attention to her habits of running her hands through her hair or of frequently moving about in her chair. She was covering her emotions well. She was intelligent and able to do her school work without any problems. Her attendance in school was good, maybe a truancy here or there, but nothing that would alarm a counselor or attendance clerk. She came from a home where her mother and father cared about their children and supported them in school. There were no indications that this girl needed help. She was a typical teenager, more mature than most, and apparently able to cope with problems in an undaunted way. One might even say her coping skills seemed to be finely tuned.

In the Monday morning "I feel" sharing sessions, Mary shared her feelings and concerns about her boyfriend, her family, and her friends. However, I noticed she was more successful in relating her concerns for others than she was in telling us what was happening to her. But she was a model peer counselor, one that was willing and able to help fellow students. Her openness in telling the class that she was seeing a therapist was instrumental in relieving the fear and anxiety of another student who had been encouraged to see a therapist.

One day near the end of the year, the class heard that Mary had checked out of school to study with a home teacher. They expressed concern immediately. "What was wrong?" Mary had looked fine on the last day of class. "Had she been in an accident?" The classroom was buzzing, but no one seemed to know the answers. Someone had reported seeing Mary's mother in the office checking her out of school that morning. But Mary was not with her mother. "Where was she?"

I listened for a moment before I interrupted the chatter. How thankful I was that Mary's mother had given me permission to tell this class about the events that had taken place over the last 48 hours.

I told the class that Mary's family had just been made aware by Mary and her therapist that she was addicted to cocaine and alcohol and that she was already checked into a drug rehabilitation hospital. The students were shocked. No one had ever guessed. Some students remembered that she had started smoking pot in junior high, like a lot of the kids had, but she was not a part of the group at high school that were known as the "party-ers." Allison, who frequently sat next to Mary, pondered, "Was I negligent as a peer counselor to not be aware of Mary's problem?"

This was not a day for business as usual in the class. If a peer counseling class is to be successful, it must be flexible.

The regular lesson plans were set aside, and I led a discussion on the importance of not feeling guilty when none is warranted. Peer counselors are not always successful in working with students even when all of the information is available to them. How could they feel guilt when they were unaware of the facts? They might feel concern, yes, but guilt, no. For whatever reason, Mary hadn't wanted the class to know before this time. The gift they had given Mary, and could continue to give her, was support and love. Maybe some day Mary would return to class and answer all of the questions the class raised. Or, maybe she would not. But for the next few months the class would support Mary with cards, letters, phone calls and, when permitted, visits.

Mary stayed in the hospital for the next eight weeks. She took her final examinations with the assistance of a home teacher, and she passed all of her classes. After leaving the hospital, Mary spent the summer at home. She attended nightly support meetings on an outpatient basis. In the fall she returned to school and graduated at mid-term, a semester earlier than the other students in her class. She immediately enrolled in the local community college, and now she was back to speak to this peer counseling class about her addiction.

Abruptly my thoughts were brought back to the present, as Mary began her personal story. Her opening remarks were spoken with warmth, understanding, and honesty, and now she was ready to share her innermost secrets.

All eyes were glued to Mary with anticipation as she began, "My family moved to Brownsboro during the middle of my first grade year, but the transition was very easy for me. I remember walking into the class and hearing the teacher say, 'Does anyone want Mary to sit next to him or her?' One girl with blond braids quickly shot her hand up and said, 'I do. I do.' And we were best friends from then until the end of sixth grade. The transition was very easy. I made friends right away, and two of my friends today are girls from that class.

"I haven't moved since that one time, so I come from a stable home life. Stable in other ways too. My parents were, and are, fine, church-going people. I learned to interact with people during those formative years because I came from a family of five kids. The house was always filled with friends and friends of friends.

"All seemed to go well in my life until I graduated from sixth grade and was promoted to junior high school. All of a sudden I felt lost. I'd been used to the security of staying in one room all day with one teacher. In junior high, as you know, we changed classes each hour, not only changing rooms but also changing teachers. I didn't have someone like the first grade teacher walking me to class and making me feel welcome. The junior high seemed huge; my elementary school had 350 students, and there were over 1000 students at the junior high. I felt overpowered. I was scared. I didn't feel like I belonged. I felt like I had a hole in my gut.

"I didn't get involved in junior high. I wasn't an athlete; I wasn't a cheerleader; I wasn't in student government; I didn't join any of the clubs on campus. My friends from elementary school were there, but there was a difference. Looking back, I think the difference was me. I migrated to a group of kids who were doing drugs, and I felt accepted. I fit right in. I didn't have to be the best athlete, the best student, or the best cheerleader. I could just be myself.

"The first time I smoked marijuana, it didn't seem to affect me. All at once I lost all my fear of drugs.The scare tactics I'd heard about marijuana, I now felt were untrue. The second or third time I smoked marijuana, it did affect me. I believe I became addicted that quickly. I never stopped after that. I was like a dog running in a circle chasing its own tail."

Tom raised his hand and Mary acknowledged him, "You said that you were addicted right away. Could you explain that?''

''Yes, I have what's called an innate addictive, obsessive-compulsive personality.''

''Is this personality inherited?'' Tom continued to probe.

''I know now that it is, but I didn't know it at the time. When I did research on my family tree, I found that my grandfather was a severe alcoholic. I had the same addictive personality he had.''

Tom nodded, and Mary continued her story.

''There I was: addicted in the seventh grade, and it went undiagnosed for four years. By the end of my seventh grade year, I had tried every drug on campus: marijuana, alcohol, amphetamines—everything, with the exception of PCP and heroin. Pills were very popular in this upper-middle class, predominantly Caucasian campus. They were easy to hide in pockets and in socks. I got into LSD, magical mushrooms, hallucinogens. By my eighth grade year, I used whatever came along. I was like a garbage can.''

I interrupted Mary this time with the comment, ''You didn't seem to have a problem getting these drugs.''

''No, there was no problem. No problem at all. I could get them on campus, at parties, in the park. If a person wants drugs, one can always find them.

''After school, or during school, it was easy to find a friend's house where both parents were at work. We could party until nearly time for the parents to come home.

''By the end of the first semester of eighth grade, I was beginning to have school problems. I was truant too many times, and my grades were dropping.

''At home the attention was on my older brother, who was rebellious at that time and causing a lot of trouble. Instead of looking at my brother and thinking, 'Wow, look what drugs and alcohol are doing to his life,' I thought, 'Look at how he has everyone going against him; he isn't doing it right.' And instead of saying drugs are bad for me and I want to stay as far away as possible, I decided to be hip, slick and cool, and beat the system before the system beat me. So I became a model kid at home. If my parents told me to be in by eleven o'clock, I always got there five minutes before eleven. I did what I was told, and I played the game.

"At school I decided to do the same thing. My friends were getting into trouble all of the time—truancies, shoplifting, parent conferences at school. I didn't want that, so I decided to work the system for me, not against me. I had always been told that I had a lot of potential, and at the end of the eighth grade, I decided to study and bring my grades up to an acceptable level for college.

"I got a part-time job, and I worked and went to school—and partied.The majority of my friends didn't graduate from junior high.That was the type of group I was running around with.

"In the summer after my ninth grade graduation, I realized I was in trouble. I would be going on to high school in the fall and that terrible feeling I had in my gut at the beginning of seventh grade came back. The fear and insecurities were there all over again. This time I didn't have the friends I had from sixth grade. In fact, I had very few friends because most of the crowd I hung out with either didn't graduate or went to continuation school. I was alone, and I was scared. But in ninth grade I had made up my mind, not only was I going to graduate from high school, but I was going to do it a semester early. I was not a quitter. I would never quit.

"So there I was in tenth grade—lost and alone in what

I perceived to be a cold, impersonal place. I got the reputation for being a loner because I didn't try to get involved with anyone or anything on campus. I was scared out of my mind. This time was different though. This time I knew how to fix the problem. This time I knew how to fill that hole in my gut. And this time I knew how to get ahead of the game. So I started using real hard.

"I started the morning off by mixing vodka with my orange juice. Every morning our family would have orange juice, so I would get up to fix it. When we sat down at the breakfast table, mine just had a slightly lighter tint. I drank it fast enough so that no one noticed. Then I would rinse my dishes and put them in the dishwasher. I always cleaned my dishes; I was a good little girl. I played the game well. Then I would brush my teeth and go to school.

"In tenth grade I found a drug that 'kicked my butt.' I found cocaine, and I loved it. I had tried it before in junior high, but it was too expensive. Now I had a boyfriend who was older, out of school, successful, and who could afford to get it for me.

"By the tenth grade I was using for a completely different reason. It wasn't for fun anymore. That is when the transition hit. I was using because I had to, not because I wanted to. It was taking a lot more to get me loaded. I went from using cocaine on week-ends, to using it every day. It wasn't getting me high; it was just getting me through the day.

"In eleventh grade I isolated myself from my peer group completely. I attended school; I worked my part-time job; and I saw my boyfriend. My parents still didn't know I was using drugs because I played the game so well. I was a model child at home. I was losing weight, but my parents didn't associate weight loss with drugs.

''Near the end of the first semester of my eleventh grade year, my counselor, who was Mrs. Sturkie, called me into her office and asked me if I'd like to be in the peer counseling class the following semester.'' Mary paused and turned to me. ''I've never known why you asked me. Why did you?''

My response was simple, ''I saw you as a loner on campus, and I thought you could use the friendship of a peer counseling class.'' I then added jokingly, ''I had great foresight. I knew I'd need a good speaker for future classes.''

Everyone laughed and momentarily released the tension of the drama being played out in the room.

Soon all eyes were back on Mary, however, and the class waited with great expectation for her to continue.

''I told Mrs. Sturkie I would like to be in the peer counseling class, and I took the permission slip home for my parents to sign. They didn't know about the class since it was new on campus, but they seemed to like what I told them about it. They signed the form.

''The rest of the story involves you. The peer counseling class kept me sane that next semester. Dr. Stewart came to class three days in a row to talk to us about drugs. The first day I could tune him out, but by the second and third day, I knew what I was hearing was important. I knew I had a problem, and I knew I didn't like the way I was living. But it was the only way of life I had known for five years. I didn't want answers. I didn't want questions. I was hitting bottom, and using wasn't working anymore. I was living a secret life, and it was getting radical. My using was not recreational. It was ugly. I was killing myself.

''The therapist I'd been seeing arranged a meeting with my parents. With my therapist there to support me, I told my parents I was a drug addict. They were totally shocked. They thought I was seeing a therapist because I was having normal teenage growing pains. With their support and encouragement, I entered the hospital and started to take hold of my life and turn it around.''

As Mary talked, Freda was listening. She sat rubbing her cold, sweaty palms together, thinking, ''Mary understands what I'm feeling.'' Later Freda would tell me her story. That day she began to question, ''Could I possibly have an addiction problem? I'm just a social user. I can quit anytime that I want to. I smoke pot on the way to school, so that I can get through those dull, boring morning classes. At noon I need a little more to get through the afternoon classes. On my way home from school I need something to help me cope with the tensions at home. Then, of course, I smoke pot and do a little coke at parties like everyone else. And I could stop if I really wanted to, but I don't want to.''

Returning from her thoughts for a moment, Freda became conscious that Mary was saying, ''You know, addicted people sometimes feel like they're in control, but they aren't.''

''How could Mary know what I was thinking,'' wondered Freda. ''Of course, she couldn't. That was only a coincidence. But am I really in control of my life or am I getting myself into deep water? My grades have dropped, and I have mood swings. I cut classes when I feel that I can't cope.''

After class was over Freda waited until several other students had talked to Mary. Then she approached Mary and asked if they could get together after school. A date was set and a peer counseling relationship began. While Freda might fool other peers, she could not fool Mary. None of the , ''If I want to stop I can'' excuses worked with Mary. She knew the symptoms of addiction all too well. She took Freda with her to an Alcoholics Anonymous meeting and to her drug abuse clinic's outpatient meetings.

It soon became apparent that Freda needed to get away from the environment she'd lived in as an abuser. She needed to be in a drug rehabilitation ward with intensive counseling and support. Her parents, whom she had confided in only recently, were very supportive. While they were shocked and alarmed and felt unwarranted guilt at the fact that their daughter needed treatment, they were anxious to meet with the staff doctor and get whatever treatment their daughter needed.

During the six weeks Freda was in the hospital, she was supported by her parents, by her peer counseling class, and by a peer alumna named Mary. Letters were written, telephone calls were made, and visiting hours were observed.

When Freda returned to school, there was one class she always wanted to attend, whether she was having a good day or a bad day. It was easy to get through all of her classes on good days; but on bad days—and there were certainly those days—she needed the peer counseling class for support. She knew they would listen when she told them she was feeling tremendous temptations to join her old crowd at lunch and light-up just one time. She had done so well up to now, but getting through the day was becoming almost unbearable for her. The class would listen. Some students who had more days of sobriety than she had would offer encouraging words and let her know that what she was feeling was normal. They told her they would be available at lunch if she would like to be with someone during the greatest hour of temptation.

The class was always there for Freda, and she stayed sober. She knew that any day of the week she could ask for the "I feel" activity where students are given the opportunity to express their feelings. While the "I feel" sessions were normally held only on Monday—and sometimes carried over to Tuesday—the students knew that if they needed to talk or to ask for support, the lesson for that day would be delayed until they were able to express their immediate concerns.

Freda expressed her feelings openly and honestly. The students listened without interrupting or giving advice. Adults do not like advice and neither do young people. When they are given the opportunity to talk without being interrupted and are allowed to arrive at their own conclusions, they develop the confidence to make wise and timely decisions. Through positive input and support from the class, Freda was able to continue to accumulate days of sobriety.

The following fall Freda received her six month sobriety chip from Alcoholic Anonymous, and I asked her to speak to the other peer counseling classes. She performed the same service Mary had, and now the snowball effect was taking place.

Tom heard Freda speak, and his story was very similar to hers. He related to what she was saying, and he entered a drug abuse program. This was peer counseling in its truest form, student A helping student B, and then student B helping student C. The students were different, but their stories were all similar.

Teachers sometimes question why we do not use just "model students" as peer counselors. Mary and Freda are good examples of students who could help other students even when they have a problem themselves. They were able to relate to students in a way a model student would have never been able to do. Conversely, a model student might be able to relate to a peer that Mary and Freda might not be able to reach. All different types of students are necessary in peer counseling because the campus is full of all different types of kids.

Mary returned to the peer counseling classes to speak on other occasions, and one day she spoke in Sue's class. Sue had been in the peer counseling program for three semesters, and she had heard other speakers talk about drug abuse. She had listened to these speakers and she had identified, but she never talked about her own excessive social using.

Sue was involved in school activities, and she was highly respected in peer counseling as a good listener and a trusted friend. She was one of the most talented writers I had ever encountered in high school. She wrote lengthy, fascinating, journals each week. Some weeks she shared her poetry with me, and I am convinced her book of poetry, when she completes it, will be published. Her grades in school were excellent, and she was accepted at a well-known university. But she did not go. She went to a drug rehabilitation hospital instead. Her plans for college have not been abandoned, just put on hold.

I received a letter from Sue after she completed her stay in the hospital. She wrote as she had written in her journals—just putting ink to her thoughts. She wrote, "I experienced the most significant and important turning point in my life as a direct result of peer counseling. I was exposed to and taught information which literally gave me hope. Hope that happiness, friends, and love were possible—possible for me."

She continued in her letter, "Specifically and personally, peer counseling exposed me to students who had been through drug rehabilitation hospitals. I realized that recovery was possible, that help was available, and that I was not alone. This realization was exactly what I needed to know at that time in my life. I sought help, and I can honestly and openly say that presently I am a recovering alcoholic and drug addict."

Sue ended her letter with, "Peer counseling clearly played, and is playing, a major role in my recovery. I have used the incredible skills I learned in peer counseling to better communicate with people who care about me. I have used the activities we did in class to help raise my self-esteem.

"Today I have self-esteem.
Today I have healthy relationships.
Today I am happy.
And thanks to you, Mary,
because you shared your story . . . .
Today I am sober."

CHAPTER THREE
Teacher—Friend or Foe?

I felt a chill race through my body as I read the lines of the journal. My eyes must be playing tricks on me. It was after 6 p.m., and I'd been working steadily since 7:30 a.m. I had taught three peer counseling classes, enrolled four new students, held two parent conferences, and seen 11 students for individual counseling.

Now the weight of the day showed in my posture as I slumped comfortably in the chair. As if to call myself to attention, I quickly sat up straight and read the paragraph once again. I hadn't been mistaken. Felicia's handwriting was bold, clear, and easy to read. In fact, it reminded me of her; the script was beautiful, and so was she. The lines on the page seemed to jump out at me. "Today Ken walked me to my class." What about this seemingly innocent statement was so startling? I rubbed my forehead and closed my eyes, trying to recall Felicia's exact words in peer counseling class two months ago—

''I feel wonderful today. I have a new boyfriend, and I think he is very special.''

The class joined in her rejoicing with, ''That's great,'' ''Super,'' ''Tell us about him.''

Encouraged by their support, Felicia continued as her dark eyes sparkled, ''He is very handsome: tall, athletic body, blond hair, blue eyes.''

I couldn't help but think what a good-looking couple they must make. Felicia was as beautiful as any magazine cover-girl. She was at least 5'9'' with the slender, lithesome body of a model. Her olive complexion, jet black hair, and big green eyes gave her the appearance of a beauty queen.

When Felicia walked into a room, she was instantly noticed. One would think she would have many boyfriends, but she had not mentioned a boy until this particular day. Now she was radiant. I could imagine her with the boy who she had just described. He was probably one of the jocks on campus who all of the girls would die to date.

My image of him faded quickly as Felicia continued, ''He is older than anyone that I've gone with before. He is 42.''

The class was silent, almost catatonic.

The rules of the class included ''no put downs'', and this rule was seldom broken. I could feel the tension in the class, and I sensed a desire of the students to question Felicia's judgment.

Richard ventured the first question. ''How do you feel about going with a man that is—uh, that age? '' he asked slowly. I felt what he really wanted to say was, ''— old enough to be your father?''

''I enjoy being with someone more mature,'' Felicia answered. ''He is kind, considerate, and we like the same things.''

"What does your mother think about him?" Ellen wanted to know.

"I haven't told her," Felicia confided. "He doesn't come to my house."

Judy, the effervescent, popular cheerleader added, "I dated a guy for a while who was five years older than me. He was a senior in college, and my mother threw a fit every time I went out with him. It got to be such a hassle I decided it wasn't worth it. Besides, I could only see him once a month when he came home for a weekend."

Henry, the ever-wise, ever-thinking student asked, "Do you sometimes wonder, Felicia, why a 42 year old man would want to go out with a 17 year old senior?"

Before Felicia could answer, Judy popped back with, "Because she is so pretty and has such a nice personality. Any man would want to go out with Felicia."

"I wasn't talking about Felicia in particular," clarified Henry. "I was thinking in general about older men dating younger women. What makes them interested in young girls?"

I noticed Felicia squirm a little in her chair, and I felt it was time to redirect the class's attention. If she were made to feel uneasy, she might never confide in them again. Since she wasn't sharing her secrets with her mother, she needed to confide in someone. The class could serve in that capacity until she felt ready to tell her mother. In fact, their sympathetic understanding and encouragement might be just what she needed to give her the courage to talk with her parents. But I knew we shouldn't push. When students are pushed, they often retreat within themselves and nothing is accomplished.

I broke into the conversation, "Henry, you've raised an interesting question, and I think the class should have the opportunity to think about it, research it, and present their findings and feelings. Today, we need to get on with the 'I feel' session, but next week, we will discuss your question as part of our unit on 'dating relationships.'''

Next week the spotlight would be off of Felicia, and we could discuss this legitimate question without her feeling each comment was directed at her. It's important that no student feel as though he or she is the guinea pig being looked at under the microscope.

Felicia seemed relieved to turn to the person sitting next to her as we continued on with the ''I feel'' session.

The following week the students held a well-prepared discussion on dating the older man or woman. We discussed the problem in terms of either girls or boys. The pros were presented first; the older dates usually have more money to spend than high school students. They can take their partners to nicer places. They aren't competing with the other girls or boys on campus, and so on. But when the class began presenting the cons, it was soon apparent that this list would be much longer.

They pointed out that differences in ages could surface conflicting interests that might not be apparent at first; that the student would be giving up part of his or her high school experience; that the older person might not be interested in high school dances; that the more experienced man or woman might have different expectations from a date; that parents would probably object; that dates might have to be kept secret. The list continued to grow as the entire class joined in the discussion.

Felicia seemed very comfortable with the discussion and offered comments pro and con. Her contributions were well-prepared, and it was apparent that she had spent a lot of time thinking about this subject.

When the discussion was over, the group had agreed that a three year age difference seemed to be the most high school students could comfortably cope with when dating. Any greater difference was almost certain to create problems.

Felicia agreed with the class by nodding along with many others, but the class seemed to sense that her intellectual approval didn't mean she agreed in her heart. Still, they didn't aim any comments directly at her, nor had they done so during the discussion.

So Felicia had not been put on the spot, and during the succeeding "I feel" sessions, she continued to express her feelings. Sometimes these involved her boyfriend; sometimes they didn't.

But I did begin to see a difference in the way Felicia looked. The change was so gradual that I didn't notice it until one day when she sat directly across from me in the circle. Her thick black hair was pulled back in a bun, and she looked a great deal older. I realized I hadn't seen her in jeans and a tee shirt for weeks. She was now wearing dresses or suits every day, with hose and heels.

Students dressing in a professional manner might appear noticeable and out of place on some campuses, but ours had so many students with individual ideas about style and taste that one was apt to see almost anything. Our only dress code was that clothing must be decent and not distracting to other students.

Since many students went directly from school to an office job, Felicia's new look certainly wasn't out of the ordinary. But I knew she didn't have a job, and I remembered she used to dress more casually, with her hair falling loosely around her face.

''Is everything all right with you, Felicia?'' I asked when class was over.

''Fine, Mrs. Sturkie,'' she answered as she gathered her books to rush to her next class. ''Thanks for asking. See you tomorrow.'' I knew her smile and manner were meant to reassure me, but I still felt uneasy.

This feeling continued for several weeks. Then I read the startling words in her journal, ''Today Ken walked me to my class.'' This made me wonder. How could a 42 year old man walk Felicia to class without being noticed and talked about? Could this 42 year old man be a teacher? The thought was disturbing, but her description of the man she called Ken did fit Mr. Saks, who taught in the math department.

Mr. Saks was very likeable. I didn't know how old he was, but would guess he was in his late thirties or early forties. He was charming, intelligent, well-dressed, and had the reputation of being a womanizer. He'd been at our school for over ten years and was well-respected as a teacher. How could I suspect him of dating a student? Mr. Saks was a professional colleague.

Still, the question lingered— ''Could Felicia's 'Ken' be Bill Saks?'' I quickly gathered up the other journals to take home and finish reading after dinner. Leaving the desk stacked with memos, class schedules, reports, and uncompleted projects, I hurried to the car and drove away, resolved not to worry about Felicia until tomorrow. After all, I would have my own family vying for my attention when I walked in the door. I felt strongly about being available for them until after dinner when they retreated to their own projects or homework.

That particular night I broke my own rules. I thought about Felicia while I was preparing dinner and while my son told me about the high-scoring forward who sprained his ankle at basketball practice that afternoon. My son interrupted my thoughts with, ''Mom, don't you understand what that means? If Wesley can't play Friday night, we'll be creamed!'' I quickly expressed my concern. I couldn't be a poor listener at home, not after having stressed in class the importance of listening with full attention. I said I hoped it was only a minor sprain and that Wesley would be suited up and ready to play on Friday night.

The following morning I arrived early at school and did some paper work before the students arrived on campus. I knew that I must send for Felicia at the beginning of first period. I had to ask her about what she'd written in her journal. I needed to relieve my mind so that I could go on to the demands of the day.

Felicia appeared at my door wearing a two-piece, blue business suit. Her hair was neatly pulled back into a bun, which seemed to emphasize her carefully-applied make-up. I looked at her and thought: ''This 17 year old girl looks like a 25 year old woman.''

After exchanging warm greetings, I got right to the point. ''Felicia,'' I said, ''I read your journal last evening, and one sentence was confusing to me. I don't understand about Ken walking you to your class.''

I knew the moment the words were out of my mouth that I had hit upon something. The color drained from Felicia's face, and as she lowered her head, her voice was almost inaudible. ''I need to talk to you, Mrs. Sturkie. I started to come to your office several times, but I haven't had the courage. I'm glad you called me in today. I need to tell someone what happened, but I can't talk to my mother. She would never understand. I'm afraid that she would think it's my fault—

and maybe it is.''

''Why don't you start at the beginning, Felicia,'' I said, as I reached for the telephone on my desk to tell the secretary to reschedule my next appointments. Somehow I knew this was going to take a while.

''The man that I am seeing is a teacher on campus,'' she began. My fear had become a reality, but I knew I shouldn't act shocked or alarmed. I encouraged her to continue.

''Tell me about it,'' I said.

Felicia poured out her story for almost an hour. It was as though a volcano had erupted and couldn't stop until all its lava had spewed out.

''I was working for Mr. Ross as his teacher's aide in math last semester,'' she began, ''and as part of my job, I entered his grades into the computer in the math workroom. One day I was working on the computer when Mr.Saks came in. He teased me about always hogging the computer, and I returned his comments with a little teasing of my own, 'Well, at least someone is working around here.'

''It started off so innocently. Mr. Saks was fun to talk to, and I felt flattered that he would come into the workroom and joke with me. He always treated me as an adult, not as just a high school senior, and I liked that. He would comment on what I was wearing; and after a while, I found myself dressing to try to please him. I stopped wearing my jeans and wore dresses and suits. I thought they made me look older.

''One day Mr. Saks commented on the way my sweater looked, suggesting he liked the way it outlined my breasts. I told him, half-jokingly, half-seriously, to go away and pick on the little tenth grade girls. He laughed and made some comment about them not having as good figures.

"I saw Mr. Saks as a harmless Casanova. He was very good-looking. I knew his reputation with women, but I felt sure he would restrict his advances to friends his own age. After all, I thought, students can trust teachers.

"Mr. Saks reminded me of my own father, who I haven't seen in over three years. My father and mother divorced when I was 10 years old, but my father always lived near by until I was 14. Then he married and moved to Florida, and I haven't seen him since."

Felicia reached for another tissue and continued, "You've never seen my father, so you can't imagine how much resemblance there is between him and Mr. Saks. I have my mother's dark hair and complexion, but I have always wanted to look like my father. I've dreamed of having his fair complexion and blond hair. I've even thought about bleaching my hair.

"And Mr. Saks jokes with me the same way my father used to. I can remember him coming home from the office when I was four or five and bringing me a candy bar. Mom would always fuss that he was spoiling my appetite and causing my teeth to decay, but he'd gather me in his arms and make up the most wonderful stories about where he had to go to find a particular candy bar meant just for me. His imaginary journeys would take me to the kitchen of little elves who knew exactly how much chocolate I liked in my candy bar. I get a warm feeling even now when I think of those days.

"When Mr. Saks started showing me attention, it was as if my father had returned—but I don't think I recognized that at the time. I just knew I enjoyed his attention. When he asked me to be his teacher's aide, I gladly accepted. I helped grade his papers, put his grades into the computer, run his tests off on the mimeograph machine, and do basically the same things I'd done before for Mr. Ross. Very soon, I found that he was giving me more work to do than I could get done, so I started staying after school to finish.

"One afternoon when I was staying late, Mr. Saks entered the workroom where I was sitting at the computer. All of a sudden he grabbed my shoulders and kissed me.

"I thought, 'Wow, this has never happened to me before. This is weird.'

"After he kissed me, he said, 'This is just between the two of us.'

"I was overwhelmed, complimented, and frightened all at the same time.

"I quickly left the room and didn't return to help him until two days later. During those two days, I replayed the scene over and over in my mind, and I was convinced by then that he really loved me. After all, this man could have any woman he wanted— so I thought—and he had chosen me to kiss. I even started to smoke during this time. I thought it made me look older and more sophisticated.

"From that point on I considered him my boyfriend, even though I never saw him any place except on campus.

"In the peer counseling class I shared my feelings about this older man, but I couldn't tell anyone who he was. I wanted to blurt the whole thing out to the class. After all, I knew it wouldn't go outside the walls of that room—confidentiality is strictly kept by everyone—but because he had been so stern in his orders to me to tell no one, I kept it to myself."

"Keeping a secret like that must have been very difficult for you," I injected.

"It was—very difficult—but he had made me promise.

"On Valentine's Day I sent him a card, and I remember signing it, 'Thanks for being my friend. Love, Felicia.'

"A few days after that I was working on his papers during my teacher's aide period, and he asked me if I would come back after school and do some more work for him. I was always happy for an opportunity to be with him, so I said, 'Yes, of course, I'll be glad to help.'

"I remember the day so well. It was raining—a real crummy day. He was helping coach the boys' basketball team, and they were working out in the gym. He told me to go on to his room and get started with the papers on his desk; he'd be there as soon as practice was over.

"I'd worked for about an hour when I heard the key turn in the door and saw him enter. He seemed to be in a very cheerful mood as he sat down beside me and started to talk. He told me how it was going to be after I graduated. He said he planned to leave the woman he was living with, and then the future would be ours together. I know you must think that I was terribly gullible, Mrs. Sturkie."

I reassured her, "You believed him, and to you it was possible."

"Yes, I definitely believed him. When he held me in his arms and promised me we would have a beautiful life together, I didn't question it at all."

At this point the tears that had been rolling down her cheeks turned into sobs. I asked her if she would like to stop and take a break. Maybe she would like a glass of water. She declined all offers except for more tissues; she stated that she would like to continue.

"He began to kiss me repeatedly, and I knew that things were getting out of hand. I was getting scared. I pulled away and told him that I had to go. It was after dark and my mom would be getting home from work soon.

"I took a couple of steps toward the door, and turned the handle. My hands were shaking, but that wasn't the reason the door didn't open. I turned the knob again, and then I realized that the door was locked. I hadn't noticed at the time, but he must have locked the door when he came in.

"As I stood there facing the door, I felt his hand on my shoulder. His other hand reached out to the light switch and turned off the lights.

"We were in the dark. There weren't any windows in the room. It was after five o'clock, and I was sure everyone else on campus had left. A shudder went through my body. He felt the quiver under his hands and he said, 'Don't be afraid. I'm not going to hurt you.'

"At that point I didn't feel like I was with a man I loved. I felt scared to death and powerless under his strong grasp. I wanted to go home. I wanted to curl up in my bed, pull the covers over my head, and make this nightmare go away.

"He was whispering that he loved me, as he lowered me to the floor.

"My knees were so weak that I felt them literally shaking as my body touched the carpet."

A shiver again went through her body as she recalled the frightening afternoon. I didn't interrupt. She had said she wanted to tell me the whole story, and as painful as it was, I must let her continue.

Her eyes looked toward the floor as she described the next few minutes. "His body felt heavy against mine, and I felt like I couldn't breathe. I tried to push away as he began undressing me, but it was useless."

"The next minutes seemed like hours—I remember crying out in pain, 'Stop! Stop! You're hurting me.' —God, how it hurt!

"Then there was a knock at the door and I heard a student's voice saying, 'Mr. Saks, you left your coat in the gym. I have it for you.'

"Before Mr. Saks could stop me, I screamed, 'He'll be right there!'

"Mr. Saks quickly got up and pulled me to my feet. Somehow I managed to get my clothing together enough to cover myself and move toward the door. When Mr. Saks opened it, I ran to the restroom so quickly I didn't even see the person who had knocked.

"Once I was in the restroom, I felt somewhat safe. I tried to pull myself together. My blouse was open, and my bra was torn. I put on my panties and pantyhose, and patted some water on my face.

"As I walked out of the restroom onto the campus, the rain came down in sheets. I didn't mind. No one on the streets would be able to see my tears as I walked home."

This time there was no rain to wash her tears away as she sat sobbing. I got up from my chair and reached out to her. Why did something like this ever have to happen, and why particularly did it have to happen on our campus, with one of our teachers?

"How long ago was this, Felicia?" I asked.

"Only two days ago. It was after I wrote my journal."

"Have you seen Mr. Saks since it happened?"

"No, I've cut my teacher's aide class both days, and I've stayed away from that part of the campus."

"Have you told your mother?"

"No, and I don't want her to ever know. I don't want anyone to ever know. It's a relief to tell you, Mrs. Sturkie, but I don't want anyone else to know. I feel so ashamed.

It must have been partly my fault."

"Felicia," I said sternly, "I want you to listen to me. You are not to blame yourself for what happened. No matter how much you felt you were in love with Mr. Saks, he is the teacher. He's responsible for watching out for your welfare and safety. A school must be a safe place for students, and teachers must never take advantage of a student. You were violated, Felicia, and you are not to blame yourself."

Guilt and blame are things that don't go away just by one person telling the other that he or she is not guilty. I told Felicia that her mother would probably want to take her to see a therapist so that she could work through her guilt feelings.

"Mrs. Sturkie," Felicia said, "You don't understand. My mother must not find out what happened. I know you won't betray my confidence."

"Felicia," I said softly, "You remember on the first day of peer counseling class, I told the entire group that everything that was said in the room would be kept confidential, with two exceptions. By law, I must report child abuse; and the other exception is that I would report any student who I felt was in a life threatening situation—for example, anyone who might be suicidal.

"I understand the pain you are having now, and I wish that I could make it go away and you wouldn't have to deal with this. But that's fantasy, not reality. I can't make your pain go away by wishing. Neither can I keep what you have told me confidential. By law, I must report child abuse; and, Felicia, this act against you was sexual child abuse."

"Please, Mrs. Sturkie," she pleaded, "Don't report this. I don't want to get Mr. Saks into trouble. He might lose his job."

"That will be up to the authorities. But even if he does, it won't be because of anything you've done, Felicia. It will be because of what he has done himself."

"Mrs. Sturkie, when you report it, does my mother have to know too?"

"Yes, Felicia, she does. And her support will be invaluable."

"I can never tell her. I can never, never do that!"

"Would you like someone else to be there with you?"

"I'd like for you to be there, Mrs. Sturkie. In fact, I'd like you to be the one to tell her. I don't even want to be in the room."

"All right, then. You can be in the room next door," I suggested. "and join us right afterwards."

We agreed that this was the way it would be handled. Although I usually feel it is best for the student to be the one to tell his or her parents any news like this, I felt that Felicia had been through enough emotionally for one day. If I could lighten the burden, I would.

Felicia and I then talked about what would happen next. I have always felt that students shouldn't be left in the dark, where things can often seem worse than they really are. So I explained every step I was going to take very carefully.

I told her I would tell my principal and my assistant principal at the same time. The principal would then call the report in to the authorities, and he would follow up his call with a written report. Next, a person from Child Protective Services (a unit of the Department of Public Social Services) or from the local police department would come and talk to Felicia. While all of this was happening, I would call Felicia's mother and ask her to come to the school.

Being a counselor is never easy, but sometimes it is harder

than others. Having to repeat the story that I had just heard would certainly be one of the hardest.

When I went into the principal's office, I looked first at the assistant principal and then at the principal. These were two men who had given me tremendous support when I began the peer counseling class. I didn't want to complicate their lives by telling them the information they were about to hear. Reporting child abuse is never pleasant, but reporting a teacher is agony. The look on my face must have told them something was seriously wrong. By the time I finished, they knew the problem was even more difficult than they had anticipated.

As hard as it was to tell the administrators, it was even harder to tell Felicia's mother. After the initial shock, she asked what she should do. I told her that Felicia needed her support and her love. We talked about how it's normal for child abuse victims to feel it's their fault and that Felicia was having some of those same feelings. We talked also about the fact that Felicia would probably need to see a therapist.

When we finished talking, I told her Felicia was waiting in the conference room next door and that I would get her.

Felicia's immediate question was, "How did she take it?"

I assured her that her mother had taken the news very well and that she wanted to support Felicia.

When Felicia and I entered my office, she immediately ran to her mother and threw herself into her mother's awaiting arms. The fear barrier had been broken, and Felicia was finding the support she so desperately needed.

During the next few days, a full police investigation was conducted very quietly. Mr. Saks was removed from school, never to return.

The police also found out that several other girls on

campus had been involved with Mr. Saks. Each girl had thought she was the only one. Faithfully, she had kept the relationship a secret, as Mr. Saks had told her to do. The parents of each girl were notified, and counseling sessions with a therapist were encouraged.

The peer counseling class never knew that Mr. Saks was the 42 year old man who Felicia had talked about in class. They did notice that Felicia was wearing jeans and looking like a 17 year old once again. She shared in the "I feel" session that she had broken up with her boyfriend, and the class seemed glad to know she had decided to go with boys her own age again.

There was some talk on campus that Mr. Saks left because he had molested some girls, but the identities of the girls was never known.

Fortunately, peer counseling was never linked to Mr. Saks' leaving. A new program certainly does not need or want that type of publicity. But the fact remains that if it had not been for a peer counseling class on campus, Mr. Saks might still be there. And the peer counseling class contributed something else. If Felicia had not been in peer counseling, she might not have had the opportunity to know her counselor well enough to trust sharing the secret with her.

Several years have passed since Felicia graduated, and she has gone on to college and a job. We have remained good friends, and only rarely does the name of Mr. Saks come up in our conversation.

While Felicia is now an apparently well-adjusted, 21 year old, I was troubled recently to hear her say, "I will not allow myself to get into a relationship unless I have complete control. I still have a fear of a strong male figure. Usually, I go out with boys who are younger than I am and are intimidated by me. Maybe some day that will change.''

Maybe some day it will, Felicia. I hope so.

CHAPTER FOUR

Pregnancy—Making the Right Choice

''I'd always thought being a peer counselor was 'my thing,''' Sally confided to her classmates. ''But now I'm having a very difficult time. I'm doubting my own abilities.'' Continuing more slowly she added, ''In fact, I don't know if I can handle this particular case.''

The class sat in silence, listening but apparently perplexed. If Sally couldn't handle a case, then who could? She was recognized by her peers as being one of the most talented peer counselors in class.

Sally sensed the class's nonverbal questions and began to explain, ''Tamara (the name I'll use to identify my counselee) asked to speak to me during brunch yesterday. I was wearing my peer counseling sweatshirt, and she approached me and said that she needed to talk to someone. She said she was new on campus, and as part of her orientation, she'd been told that the students wearing the peer counseling sweatshirts would listen and help if she ever needed assistance.''

Sally glanced around and noted that she had everyone's undivided attention. She then continued, ''Tamara had such a scared, lost look on her face that I decided I'd skip lunch with my friends and offer to eat with her.

''We agreed to get our lunches from the cafeteria and meet under the tree by the girls' athletic field. I explained to her other students seldom visit that part of the campus during lunch, and we'd be able to talk without interruption.

''When Tamara arrived she didn't have her lunch with her. She said she really didn't feel like eating. Her face looked so drawn and pale that I insisted she take my apple.

''I'd never seen this girl before today, but a rapport developed quickly between the two of us. She seemed so relieved to have someone to listen to her, and listen is just what I did. I didn't interrupt her story. I just listened, nodding when it was appropriate to let her know that I understood what she was saying. I'll try to replay the scene for you just as it happened—.

''Tamara began, 'I'm new to this school, and I want to be accepted so badly. I feel left out of everything here. I was popular at my last school, and I miss my friends so much. Anyway, the reason I'm telling you this is so maybe you can understand how I got myself into this mess.'''

Since the class had not seen Tamara, Sally began to describe the girl so they could see her as she had. ''Tamara wasn't a pretty girl, but she seemed to have a knack for doing the most with what she had. She was wearing designer jeans with a shirt and sweater, and they were all coordinated in a manner that showed she was aware of fashion. Her hair was cut in the latest trend, short on one side and longer, curled under on the opposite side. She dressed and looked like many of the other kids on this campus.

"I was confused as to why this girl felt so left out," Sally continued, "and the confusion must have shown on my face because Tamara anticipated my question before I asked it. She said, 'I know you're wondering why I feel left out at your school when it seems so friendly here to you. That's the way I felt at my old school. I couldn't understand how anyone could ever feel left out there, but looking back now, I'm sure a lot of kids did.'"

"I nodded, and Tamara continued, 'The school I came from was in a small, rural town, and my dad was the pastor there of a conservative church. I was accepted at the school immediately because my parents were highly regarded in the town, and that respect filtered down to me. Everyone knew everyone else, and it wasn't difficult to be popular.

"'When we moved to this city, I found the neighborhood feeling that I was used to didn't exist, and the kids at school didn't even know or apparently care that my dad was the pastor of a local church. At least, it didn't open any doors for me as it did before.'

"Tamara spoke in a hurried voice as if she wanted to give me all of the information she could before telling me the real reason she wanted to talk to me. I listened as she continued with background information, 'My mother and father always protected my sister and me. I often thought we were overprotected. We have to be in by 10 p.m. on weekdays, and never later than midnight on weekends. Our religion frowns on drinking or smoking, so, being the pastor's kid, I certainly was never allowed to do those things. And I really didn't mind. There were always things to do at church, a lot of youth activities: dances, camping trips, picnics. I didn't need to drink or smoke to be popular at school. There was a group that partied, but they weren't really the popular kids.

"'I may be mistaken, but it seems like everyone at this school parties, and there aren't any parties where the kids don't drink. The first time I went to an open party a girl in my civics class told me about, I just stood around all evening and watched. It was so different from our church socials. I wished I could go back where I fit in, but that was impossible. Dad's new congregation consists mostly of retired people, and there isn't even a youth director on staff.

"'The next party I went to was the one that got me into so much trouble.'"

"'Trouble with your parents?' I asked."

"'On, no, they don't even know I went to a party that night, and I originally hadn't planned on going.

"'Jill, the girl in my civics class that I told you about, invited me to spend the night at her house. She told me her parents were out of town and she didn't want to stay in the house by herself. I was so anxious to have a friend that I wanted to help Jill in anyway I could.'"

"You spent the night away without your parents' permission?" Sally asked Tamara. "I was thinking she was another student who was having problems with her parents.

"'Oh, no,' Tamara responded. 'I asked my parents. I just didn't tell them that Jill's parents were out of town and we'd be in the house alone.'

"She continued, 'About seven o'clock Jill suggested that we go out for hamburgers, and on the way back Jill wanted to cruise the neighborhood to see if we'd see any parties going on. I wasn't accustomed to crashing parties, but Jill assured me that most of them were open in this community.

"'It wasn't long before Jill pulled up in front of a house

with a lot of activity in the front yard and apparently in the house. I think Jill had been at this house before because she seemed to feel right at home. There were two kegs of beer in the kitchen and bottles of vodka, gin, and tequila on the bar. Jill took a glass of beer from the boy standing by the kegs and pushed it into my hand. Then she took a glass for herself.

"'I don't know why I did what I did, except that I remembered how lonely and out of place I'd felt at the last party, and I didn't want to feel that way again. I put the glass to my lips and took a sip. It tasted awful, but I couldn't let the others know I'd never had a glass of beer before in my life. Soon I didn't notice the taste, and I took the second and then the third glass that someone placed in my hand. I really don't remember much after that. I do faintly recall a boy standing at the bar urging me to try tequila. I guess I did. I seem to remember taking the glass. After that I don't remember anything about that night.

"'The next morning I woke up feeling sicker than I'd ever felt in my life. I didn't know where I was because the room didn't look familiar. I was shivering under the sheet. At first I thought I was shivering because my head hurt so badly and I was so nauseated, but then I realized that I was cold because the sheet was the only covering I had—and I was naked. I was very groggy, but I woke up quickly when I stretched my arm and touched someone in the same bed with me. I don't know to this day who he was. I just remember seeing an unshaven face that I didn't recognize. I don't think that he was a student at our school; at least, I'd never seen him on campus before, and I still haven't. I was lying in bed next to a total stranger.

"'I found Jill asleep in the hallway. Sleeping next to her

was a boy I recognized as being a student at our school. Apparently very few kids left the party that night. It looked like everyone was still there, sleeping on the floor, on the couch, in chairs, in hallways, on beds. I'd never seen anything like it. The parents who lived in the house were obviously away for the week-end.'''

Sally stopped telling Tamara's story to inject, "I felt a deep wave of sympathy come over me. What a terrible thing to happen to this nice girl, and no wonder she needed a peer counselor. I told her how sorry I was, and that I understood.

"Tamara responded that I didn't, and that there was more to tell.

"I reached out and touched Tamara's arm, and assured her that I was trying to understand, and wanted her to go on.

"'That happened two months ago, and now I think that I'm preg—, pregnant.' She stumbled over the word, as if saying it were too painful for her.

"'Have you you been to the doctor or a clinic to check out your suspicions?' I asked .

"'No, that's why I needed to talk to you. I overheard another girl say that peer counselors have lists of reputable agencies that might be able to help.' I asked her if she could see her family doctor and she replied, 'We don't have a family doctor because no one in the family has been sick since we moved here, and we haven't needed one. Besides, I don't want my parents to find out. You can imagine what it would do to my family's reputation in the church community.

"'If you are pregnant, then you will want your family's support, won't you?' I probed.

"'No, I don't want my parents to ever find out about this. I love them too much to hurt them in any way. I have already thought this out carefully. If I am pregnant, I want an abortion. We studied the laws relating to minors in civics class, and I know that legally I can get an abortion without telling my parents.'''

Sally went on to explain her situation to the class, ''I realized that Tamara was determined, and legally she had a right to do what she was proposing, but I didn't want her to make a quick decision she might regret later. I knew if I gave her the phone numbers of a couple of reputable agencies she could get counseling and be told about all her options. If I didn't refer her to one of the agencies on the list, then she would look in other places, and she might end up going to a clinic that was only in business to make money. We've learned in this class that the ones in business just to make money pressure the girls into getting abortions, sometimes even with false-positive pregnancy tests. Unfortunately, I heard about a girl on our campus who chose a clinic that does abortions on demand without any counseling, and now the girl is still questioning her decision.

''I told Tamara that I could give her the names of a couple of agencies, and that she'd need to choose one and then make an appointment to be sure she really was pregnant.

'''I'm nearly certain that I am,' Tamara said. 'I have all the symptoms, even down to morning sickness.' She continued, 'I don't need just the name of an agency though; I need a way to get there. I don't have a car, and if I take the bus after school I'll get home much too late. Would you please take me?'

''This is when I really began to doubt my capabilities as a peer counselor,'' Sally confided to the class.

'''Wouldn't it be better to confide in your parents and let them help you?' I asked Tamara. I know that I was on the edge of giving advice, but I thought of my own parents and knew that I could never have an abortion and not tell them. In fact, I realized that I could never have an abortion at all. That would really be against my value system.

"Luckily, the bell sounded and lunchtime was over. I was saved from having to go any further with Tamara at that point. I told her I would meet her at the same time tomorrow, and I would have my referral list with me. Tamara seemed relieved when I told her that; she said she was glad she had begun to deal with the problem instead of ignoring it as she had tried so hard to do for the past two weeks.

"This conversation took place yesterday," Sally said worriedly, "and soon I will be meeting her again. I need some input from the class. I've given out telephone numbers before, but I haven't been asked to take someone to a clinic. I've never been to one myself. In fact, I'd feel very strange just being seen there."

One of the reasons it's important to have peer counselors meeting in a class each day with a teacher present is so the peer counselors don't feel they're alone in counseling peers. Sally needed to be reminded by the teacher that a peer counselor never has to deal with a situation which makes her feel uncomfortable or is against her own values. I reminded Sally she could tell Tamara that peer counselors do not pass judgment on anyone, and that she wasn't judging Tamara, but her values didn't allow her to take someone to a clinic. She could introduce Tamara to another peer counselor. This had been done at other times when one peer counselor felt, for whatever reason, that he or she would rather not work with a particular counselee.

Jane had been listening attentively. "I'll be glad to go with Tamara," she told Sally. "I've worked with other students in similar situations, and I feel very comfortable doing it."

Sally thought carefully for a few moments and then said, "No, but thank you, Jane. I want to continue being her peer counselor. Even though I wouldn't want to have an abortion myself, I don't feel that they are morally wrong. I would like to see Tamara go to a clinic and receive counseling and make up her own mind. We have learned, as peer counselors, that we don't impose our views or our values on anyone else. We don't give advice; we only help other peers to see their options and make their own decisions, after all the alternatives have been explored, without applying any pressure."

Turning back to the class, Sally said, "Thank you, everyone. I just needed to talk this one through and listen to myself as I talked. By listening, you have helped me sort out my own feelings."

The peer counseling class continued to support Sally as she helped Tamara during the next few weeks. Tamara received counseling at the clinic by qualified counselors, and all of the options were presented to her. Abortions were not done at the clinic she went to, so there was no undue emphasis placed on them. However, if a person decided an abortion was the option that she chose, a referral could be made to one of several reputable hospitals or clinics.

According to Sally, there was no doubt in Tamara's mind as to what she wanted. She didn't feel she was ready to become a parent, nor did she want to go through the pregnancy and give up the child. Some day, she wanted children, but only after she had completed her education and had chosen a husband who would be a good father. For her child, she wanted a secure, happy family life similar to her own. But most of all, she wanted to forget that dreadful night—the night of the black-out.

Later that week, as Sally was relating to the class that Tamara had definitely decided to have the abortion, Fran quietly began to sob. One of the benefits of sitting in a circle is that emotions do not go undetected. No one is looking at the back of heads, as is the case in some regular classrooms.

As soon as Sally had finished her sentence, she turned to Fran and said softly, "Fran, have I said something to offend you? If I have, I'm sorry."

Fran reached for a tissue and looked upward, "I guess I'm just easily upset these days."

"Is there anything we can do to help?" Brett inquired.

"No, there's nothing anyone can do."

"Would you like to talk about it?" Sally gently probed.

"I've hesitated to tell you because this class is like my family, and I don't want you to think badly of me."

"Who could ever think badly of you?" Mary asked. "You are one of the sweetest, most considerate girls I've ever met."

Fran blushed a light shade of pink as she shifted uncomfortably in her chair, twisting the tissues with her fingers.

"I do try to be a nice person," Fran confessed, "but you know the saying, 'Nice girls get caught—.' Well, I got caught. I'm pregnant."

There was a deadly hush in the room, and I sensed that the students were unable to react in their role as peer counselors and come up with the right thing to say to Fran.They were stunned. Fran was probably the last girl anyone in the class would expect to be pregnant.

Fran was a girl with an almost heavenly glow. Her golden blond hair cast a halo around her angelic face. She was every girl's ideal of a trusted friend and every boy's image of a sister to be protected.

Breaking the deadly silence, Sarah said in a nonjudgmental voice, "Are you positive you're pregnant, Fran?"

"Oh, yes," Fran confirmed, "I've already been to our family doctor, and he has told me that all the tests are positive."

"You said you went to your family doctor. Are you saying that your parents know?" Steve inquired.

"Yes, I have a very good relationship with my parents, and I told my mother after I was almost certain myself." Her voice dropped, and she continued, "She was so shocked. I will never forget the look on her face. She had so much trust and faith in me, and I really let her down."

The tears began to swell in Fran's eyes as she spoke of her mother, "She has been so supportive though, and so has my father."

Sally reached for the box of tissues and placed a dry one in Fran's hand.

"I've already worked it out with my family. I'm going to marry Phil."

Before Fran could continue, John's strong voice interrupted, and the entire class saw the incredulous look on his face, "You're going to get married?" This was not the tone or type of question John had learned to use as a peer counselor. This was the shocked voice of a friend who was hearing something he could not believe.

"Yes, Phil has been out of high school for a year now, and he'll be quitting college and going to work. My family is completely opposed to abortions and so is his family."

"How do you feel about it?" Sally wanted to know.

"I feel the same way about abortions that my family does. In our church, having an abortion is a sin; and I could never, never live with myself if I killed my child. That would be too much guilt for me to bear.''

''What about Phil? How does he feel about quitting college and getting a job?''asked Jack. One could feel the pain in Jack's voice at the very thought of having to give up college for any reason. Jack had applied to the Ivy League colleges and was expecting to receive acceptances to at least two and maybe more.

''Phil isn't exactly ecstatic about it, but he doesn't believe in abortion either. His Dad has offered him a job at his hardware store. It isn't the career Phil had in mind, but maybe some day he can go back to school and become the lawyer he wants to be.''

''It sounds as if you've thought this through very carefully.'' Jack injected. Fran nodded as Jack continued, ''But have you thought of all of the options? There are alternatives other than abortion or marriage.''

''If you are thinking of adoption, I've already considered that, and really it isn't an option for me. I'm the type who would always worry if my baby were being treated well. I'd never have a night's sleep without wondering if he or she was all right. No, that really isn't an option.''

''Many unmarried girls decide to keep their babies and remain single,'' Sally added.

''My parents told me that they would help me raise the baby if I wanted to do that, but Phil's family doesn't want their grandchild to be raised without the benefit of marriage and the family name. They're pillars of their church community, and that would present a problem for them.''

''But what do you want, Fran? What is your choice?'' Sally probed.

''I want to get married. I've known Phil for nearly a year now, and he's the only boy I've ever loved.'' Fran thought for a moment and then continued slowly and thoughtfully. "I wouldn't be pregnant if I hadn't thought I really loved Phil and that he loved me."

"Have you set a date for your wedding?" June asked anticipatingly. June had been a bridesmaid in her sister's wedding only recently, and she had shared with the class at that time how much she loved weddings.

"We will be married in the church two weeks from Saturday. It will be a morning wedding, and I'll wear my mother's wedding dress. She has talked about my wearing her dress ever since I was a little girl, and I wouldn't want to disappoint her." As almost an afterthought, she added, "It's a beautiful dress."

The discussion continued with the class asking questions but never giving advice. Not giving advice was one of the hardest lessons most students had to learn. It was so natural to say, "If it were me, I'd do it this way."

Erin had sat quietly without saying a word during the entire discussion. At a pause in the conversation, she blurted out, "I can understand what you're feeling, Fran. I can understand only too well." She continued more thoughtfully and deliberately, "I'm sure a lot of you are thinking but not saying, 'If it were me, I'd get an abortion. Who wants to have a baby when she's a junior in high school!' I used to think the same way. It's easy for people who aren't pregnant to say right off that they would have an abortion. But when you're pregnant, it's hard to think about abortion. It's hard to even realize that you're pregnant. Everything is hard when you're pregnant."

All eyes were on Erin now, and the students seemed to sense what was coming next. Erin continued, "I was pregnant this time last year, and I got an abortion. I didn't have strong feelings about not getting one, and it seemed like the logical thing to do. But now there are times I think about what I did, and I know I will never have another abortion. If I ever become pregnant again I'll keep the child. I don't want to go through those feelings ever again of hating myself for becoming pregnant at a time when I couldn't have a child.''

The bell sounded, and the looks on the students' faces seemed to say what they had verbalized at other times, ''Why did that bell have to ring; there is never enough time in this class.'' Their looks in my direction were only momentary,then quickly they got up and went to Erin and Fran, offering hugs and words of support. I, too, gave hugs to both and offered invitations to talk with them individually in my office if they wanted to continue. An important role of the teacher is to assure that the students don't leave with their emotions up in the air.

During the next week, Fran kept everyone up-to-date on her wedding plans. She had selected the songs that would be sung, and her parents had decided to have the reception in the church's social room.

On a day when Fran wasn't in class due to a doctor's appointment, the students quickly planned a wedding shower for her. Students contributed any amount of money they could afford. It would be presented to Fran to purchase whatever was most needed for the apartment she and Phil would call home. Fran had told the class that each set of parents was giving them a month's rent for the little garage apartment she and Phil were so excited about finding. She was relieved to know that they wouldn't have to live with either of their parents.

The shower was held the last day Fran was in class before

her wedding. Tom and Hal had brought orange juice and milk for everyone to share, and Sally, Erin, and Mary had each baked cookies the previous night. A festive mood permeated the room, and the heaviness of the previous weeks seemed to have lifted. Fifty-two dollars had been collected, and Sally presented it to Fran with a card signed by each member of the class. Fran was visibly touched by the display of affection and caring from her classmates. She thanked each person individually, as she reached out with smiles and hugs.

During the previous weeks, the class had listened to Fran, allowed her to express her feelings without interruption, been nonjudgmental, helped her explore the options, and then supported her in her final decision. Whether that decision was right or wrong was not for the class to decide. The decision was Fran's, and it was one for which she would always claim ownership. No matter what happened in the future, Fran would remember that the peer counselors had supported and cared about her during a very difficult period in her life.

After the wedding and a very brief honeymoon, Fran returned to school to complete the last semester of her junior year. Having a married student in class was something new to the peer counselors, and they learned through Fran's Monday morning "I feels" that married life involved meeting bills, cooking meals, and washing clothes, as well as keeping up with school homework.

A baby girl was born in the early fall, and Fran stayed home with her new baby during the first semester of her senior year. She took her classes through independent study and told me that she looked forward to returning at the beginning of the second semester to complete high school and graduate with her class.

Fran returned to school as scheduled. She had made arrangements with her mother to care for the baby at her house during school hours.

The class welcomed Fran back, and she responded by saying, "It's great to be back. I have the same warm, secure feelings I've always had from being with you." The seniors from the previous year had graduated, and students who had been in the beginning peer counseling class had progressed to this advanced class. Even with new people in the class, among some of the original ones, very soon Fran was able to pick up where she left off.

The students were excited about seeing snapshots of the baby Fran so proudly passed around the room. There was no doubt in anyone's mind that Fran was an excellent mother. She spoke lovingly of her little daughter and told of the pain she felt having to be away from her all day.

Before long, Fran began to show signs of fatigue. She shared with the class that she wasn't getting much sleep—the baby was up often during the night. Because Fran was at school all day, she wasn't able to take naps in the daytime while the baby slept. When she got home in the afternoon, she had to cook dinner, wash the clothes, clean the apartment, and take care of the baby. After dinner when the dishes were washed and put away, she still had to bathe the baby, get her to bed, and then start on her school work. When asked if Phil helped with the household chores, she shared that he was having a difficult time adjusting to his job at the hardware store. She said she didn't want to pile more work on him when he got home.

When the senior prom came along and the girls were talking excitedly about their new long dresses and their dates,

Fran often had a wistful look in her eye. But she never complained. Whenever she mentioned that she and Phil were quarreling more frequently, she would add, ''But it's probably just because we are both so tired. Things will be better after I graduate.''

The class was always there to listen and support. Fran confided to me one day, ''I don't know what I'd do, Mrs. Sturkie, if I didn't have this class. They listen, and I need desperately to have this opportunity to talk and share my feelings. I can't keep my feelings bottled up inside of me, and this class is my only outlet. I can't talk to Phil because he has enough problems of his own, and I can't let my parents know that things aren't going well in my marriage. My dad's health isn't good, and if I shared my problems, I'd only be giving them something else to worry about.''

''Have you and Phil thought of talking to a marriage counselor or to your priest?'' I inquired.

''I've asked Phil if he would go with me to see our priest or to a marriage counselor, but he won't. Phil has never learned to express his feelings to another person, and the very thought of it scares him. He won't even talk to me about his feelings, but I think he blames me for his having to work at a job he doesn't like, instead of being in college.''

Near graduation time Fran did confide in the class that she and Phil were talking to a marriage counselor. She hoped their problems would soon be worked out.

Fran graduated with her class, and over a year passed before she and the other peer counselors got together again. During the summer while many of the students were home from college, Sally spearheaded a reunion.

Again, Fran had volumes of pictures to pass around, showing the baby walking, sleeping, eating, taking a bath.

There was a brightness about Fran's face everytime she mentioned the baby's name. There was no doubt that this baby was the most important thing in her life.

When it was Fran's time to share, she related that her marriage had not worked out, not even with marriage counseling. She and Phil were divorced; he was living with his parents and going to college. She was living with her parents, and her mother was taking care of the baby so she could work as a salesperson in a department store. She jokingly told the class, "Working in a department store has its merit because I'm able to use my discount to buy clothes for the baby." She hastily added, "I never knew babies outgrew their clothes so quickly."

Fran seemed to sense the question that everyone wanted to ask but would not. Her face still had that angelic glow as she spoke, "I know you are wondering how I feel about my decision—the one I made when I found out I was pregnant. Would I make the same decision today I made then? The answer is yes. I still feel I made the decision that was right for me. I won't lie. It has been hard, sheer hell at times; but I have my baby, and she means the world to me."

As others shared lighter experiences that had happened over the past year, there was a lot of laughing and joking. Jack, after spending a year at Yale, confessed to the class that for the first time in his life, he had been reduced to studying on week-ends. With good-natured kidding, Hal played his imaginary violin and said, "Poor Jack, I really feel for you." To which Jack responded, "Not only did I study on week-ends, but I still made a 'C' in physics." Laughter filled the room, and the closeness of the class was again evident.

Sally talked about her witty roommate at college and the good-looking boys on campus. I watched Fran's face lose its glow as Sally talked about dates, football games, and term papers. In place of the glow there seemed to be a wistfulness for the carefree days that Sally was describing. The two girls were the same age, but their worlds were light years apart.

When Sally glanced in Fran's direction, she changed the subject.

"Remember Tamara, my counselee who almost caused me to turn in my peer counseling shirt and admit failure? Well, I saw her last week. I ran into her at the post office, and we went to lunch together. She's working in an insurance office."

Sally continued, "Tamara asked me if there was a peer counseling class at my college, and I told her not yet, but that I'm working on getting one started. She thanked me again for being a friend when she needed one, and then she said, 'Sally, I really appreciated your nonjudgmental attitude. I knew you didn't agree with my decision because your values were different from mine, but you didn't lecture me or try to convince me to change my mind. I look back now and think how fortunate I was to have a peer counselor to help me with my problem. I wasn't emotionally mature enough to go through a pregnancy or to have a child. I know I made the only decision that was right for me at that time in my life.' Then her voice dropped almost to a whisper as she added, 'But there isn't a month goes by that I don't think about how old my child would be now if I hadn't interrupted my pregnancy.'"

Fran sat silently for a moment, and then she spoke. "Tamara and I had a similar problem, and we each dealt with it in a way that was right for us individually. But neither one of us made our decision without paying a high price."

The class sat quietly for a moment before going on to the next person. As we each thought about what had been shared in the room that day, I wondered if the peer counselors realized how many lessons about life they had taught each other.

By giving, they truly had received.

CHAPTER FIVE

Self-Esteem—Everyone a Winner

The classroom atmosphere wasn't always heavy. It wasn't always filled with the traumas of drugs, sexual abuse, abortion, and pregnancy.

My thoughts traveled back to my first day as a peer counseling teacher and the lighter side of the class. As the very first peer counseling class filed into the room on an early Monday morning, I looked at the different faces crossing the threshold. These twenty-five students had been hand-picked from personal interviews. They would be trained to become the first peer counselors on campus. The future of the entire peer counseling program at our school was in their hands. If these students received something important from the class and became effective peer counselors then the program would be a success. If they were disappointed with the class, soon the word would spread on campus, and no one would sign up for the next semester.

Unlike many of the other classes on campus, the teacher

was not the one most important person in the class. True, she would instruct the students on skill development and set the standards and climate for the class, but she would not be the focal point. By stepping back, she would allow the spotlight to be on the individual students. If a teacher felt the need for controlling at all times and lecturing every day, then this class would not be right for him or her.

Because so much learning was to take place from students helping each other, having the right combination of students in class was imperative, also impossible to predict. If a teacher wanted to teach an honors math class, then he or she would restrict that class to students who were motivated and talented in math. However the peer counseling class was created on the opposite premise.

This would not be a homogenous group all working together with one common goal. This would be a class composed of students who did not always look alike, sometimes spoke with different accents, and were miles apart in abilities and motivations. Some would be in the class because they were "well-put-together" and were capable of helping their peers. Others would be there because they were "falling apart" and needed to learn how to help themselves. What made me think a class like this would ever work? Not only might it not work, but it could be disastrous.

The chairs were already placed in a circle, and the students soon were seated. As I called the roll, I took particular note of some students: Carmen, the president of the senior class, was probably the best known student in the circle. Having a leader on campus who was eager to take part in peer counseling certainly added respectability to this new class. Hong, the muscular linesman for the football team, sat next to Carmen. The handsome, Oriental boy looked like he had met his match in the game last Friday night. The scrapes and bruises were apparent on his bare arms.

Across the circle sat Faye, a girl with straight brown hair and thick glasses. She appeared shy, and my heart went out to her. Later I would learn that she was very fearful about how she, a handicapped girl, would be received in this class.

Linda, the unmistakable cheerleader with the short, pleated skirt and sweater with the school initials, sat next to Faye. Her bubbling personality came forth as she answered to her name being called from the roll. Her brown eyes sparkled. This black girl was one of the most popular students on this predominantly white campus.

Max, a boy as well-known on campus as Carmen or Linda, but in a negative way, was leaning back in his chair with his arms folded across his chest. Max had a reputation for being a troublemaker. He would push teachers to the limits of their patience; his attendance was fair to poor; he didn't like school, and he let everyone know about it.

Sitting next to Max was Juan, a boy who was attending our school on an inter-district transfer from a school where he had been involved with a Chicano gang. He was allowed to attend our school after he had tried to break away from the gang but was beaten up on three separate occasions.

Olga had arrived in the United States only recently, and she answered to her name with a strong Norwegian accent. Everything was new to Olga—a new country, family, school, and certainly in the days to come, new friends.

Sitting side by side were two girls I couldn't tell apart, even though they answered separately as their names were called. How interesting it would be for the class to learn how identical twins really feel—do they ever find themselves with a crush on the same boy? What happens when one gets invited to the prom and the other doesn't?

I called the name Crystal twice and got no response. "Crystal Blaylock," I said loudly and clearly. Finally, a very soft voice answered, "Present."

Seeing the girl who answered reminded me of what I'd heard other teachers say about her.

"Why are you allowing Crystal to take peer counseling?" a science teacher wanted to know. "She won't add anything to your class. I had her for two semesters last year, and I bet she didn't say three words the entire time. When I'd ask her a question, she would just sit there and shake her head." Almost as an after-thought she added, "But she did know the answers because she did well on written tests."

Somehow, I knew on that first day of class that Crystal had a lot to say, and if she gained the trust of these kids, she would talk in class.

Crystal sat next to Jennifer. Maybe Jennifer would become her friend. At least, she wouldn't be overwhelmed by Jennifer, who was often referred to, in a positive way, as being very average. Jennifer never made any waves in any of her classes, she was just there.

Average is a word that Jack would have bristled at hearing if it were ever intended to describe him. Jack did everything so above-average, so outstanding, that I wondered if he'd been competing for the number one spot all of his life. I could visualize him as a baby in diapers crawling across the finish line first in a "Mr. Perfect Baby" contest. Getting him to listen to others, instead of advising them, was going to be a real challenge for me.

I finished reading the other fourteen names, put my roll sheet aside, and began class.

"Welcome to peer counseling," I said with a smile. "I want to compliment you on your intelligence. How do I know you're intelligent? You signed up for this class, didn't you?" The tension of the first few minutes of a new class faded as everyone laughed.

I continued in the same light-hearted manner. "I want to commend you for your courage. You're taking a class that hasn't been offered on this campus before; therefore, I know you haven't been able to gather information from classmates as to whether this class is good or bad. You're taking a risk. How courageous!

"I want to compliment you on your caring personality. This class was described to you as one that would train you to help other students and yourself. If you didn't care about your peers or yourself you wouldn't be here.

"I have just commended you for having three traits that are shared by people who are known as winners—they are intelligence, courage, and compassion. I believe that each of you has these qualities. One student may have more of one and less of another than the student sitting next to him, but each of you has all of these traits.

"You are all winners! And as winners you deserve to be treated with respect. I will treat you with respect and dignity; and I, in turn, expect you to treat each person in class in the same way.

"You are here because you each have been chosen to be one of the twenty-five out of sixty students who will be in this first peer counseling class. Because you were chosen and someone else was not, makes you a winner already. We have a class of twenty-five winners!"

As I said these words and began a journey to build self-esteem to a greater degree in each student, I was unaware of the extent to which these kids would really be winners. They were going to live up to those words, and each would wear the banner of a winner well.

During the first week of class, we all worked on the unit entitled "Building Social Ease." This was a good unit to start with because it enabled the students to get to know each other while at the same time learning to reach out and talk to strangers.

The first exercise we did was to give each person the opportunity to describe himself. Going clockwise around the circle, each one had as little or as much time as he or she wanted to speak. There was never pressure put on anyone, and if a person didn't want to share, that person only had to say, "I pass" and no questions were asked.

Several students had already spoken when it came Faye's time to speak.

"I have a few problems," she began, "but nothing I can't handle."

That was the only comment she made regarding her physical handicaps. I was to learn later that she had been born prematurely, and for the first few days, wasn't expected to live. Her good brain and great spirit were to dwell in a body that had been afflicted with a cerebral disorder. Surgery would help her to walk, with one foot hesitating behind the other. Thick lenses would give her vision to see, but would not allow her to read books or write at the same speed that other students did.

"Drama is my favorite subject," Faye continued, "and I'm looking forward to being in some plays this year."

The rest of the description of herself was on the same upbeat note. She didn't need or want sympathy from anyone. I had a good feeling that this student was going to be a "giver" instead of a "taker."

My first impressions were correct. As the weeks went by, Faye gave all of us new insights. While her vision was limited, her hearing was very acute. She amazed the students by being able to remember all the names after hearing them only once. She also listened well with what we call a "third ear." She seemed to be able to perceive what the person was not saying by listening "between the lines."

In the following months, Faye was able to do the required two book reports, but when it came time to do her main project for the semester, she worried about what to do. Each student had been given a choice to find a project of particular interest to him or her that would also benefit someone else.

Faye had helped Tom carry out his project, as had the entire class. Tom had chosen to have a luncheon for the teachers, hoping to present a program that would further spread the good word about peer counseling. As hard as it was for the students to understand, the fact remained that there were a few teachers on campus who were still skeptical about peer counseling.

Led by Tom, the students had set up the activity center with tables and chairs, decorated the room, and brought food for a potluck meal.

Faye was one of the four after-lunch speakers, and several of the teachers told me later that she had brought tears to their eyes as she told them how much it meant to her to have twenty-four friends who were accepting and caring.

Even though Faye had helped Tom with the teachers' luncheon, she still needed to find her own project. The day she bounced into the room, waving a sheet of music in her hand, I knew she had found it.

''Mrs. Sturkie, Mrs. Sturkie,'' she said excitedly, ''I've found my project. I'd like to organize the class into a choir and present a program of Christmas carols to the patients at the convalescent hospital. Doesn't that sound super?''

I assured her that it did—I would never squelch enthusiasm like that—but I had a few reservations. The hospital was located just down the street from the school, but it was very large, covering three stories. I wanted each student to be successful in his or her project, and I wondered if what Faye had proposed was too big a job for her.

It wasn't. She made copies of Christmas carols, distributed them to the students, and let them know that she expected them to learn the words and music. Faye loved to sing, and she was able to bring that joy to the rehearsals.

The class sounded so professional on the day before the performance that I was amazed. Now everyone was proud to be a part of Faye's project. One boy volunteered to wear a Santa suit, and three other students volunteered to bring candy canes for him to pass out to the patients and nursing staff.

Faye arranged with the principal for the ''choir'' to sing to the school office staff at noon on the day of the scheduled performance. Max jokingly said that he had never been to the office except when he was in trouble. Faye responded, ''Well, it's time you're seen in there doing something positive.'' Max wasn't sure he wanted to be seen singing carols, but turning down Faye was something not even Max would do.

The office staff applauded loudly, and the peer counselors felt encouraged to go on to their next performance, which would be after school at the hospital.

This was Faye's project, and she proved to be, not only

a capable singer, but also an effective leader. ''Jingle Bells,'' ''Santa Claus is Coming to Town,'' and ''Silent Night'' were heard throughout the hospital. The patients who were able to be up, as well as others in wheelchairs, were eager to join in singing along with the young people. Faye became so confident that she asked the patients to request their favorite songs. Fortunately, their requests were well-known favorites. Santa Claus passed out candy canes, after receiving permission from the head nurse.

Without a doubt in anyone's mind, Faye's project was a big success.

The next day in class, Faye beamed as different students told how meaningful the previous day had been to them. After that project, Faye was the recognized ''choir director'' in the class. And when anyone had a birthday, the class looked to Faye to lead them in singing a ''Happy Birthday'' salute.

Faye was a winner.

Like Faye many others came to amaze us all and surprise even themselves.

During the first week that Olga was in the peer counseling class, she shared with the students that it had been her dream for many years to come to the United States as a Norwegian exchange student. Her older sister had been an exchange student in New Jersey, and hearing about life in America whetted her appetite for a similar adventure.

I had always felt a real concern for exchange students. I had seen some arrive with such anticipation and high hopes, only later to see their eagerness replaced with discouragement and homesickness. Being away from home for such a long period sometimes brought feelings of regret about having made the trip. This seemed especially true when the personalities of the host family were not compatible with the student's. Moving to another host family often produced its own feelings of failure and frustration.

I felt that being in a peer counseling class where feelings could be talked out would be very helpful to these students. Now with Olga I would have an opportunity to see.

Olga had a delightful personality. Her openness and candidness enabled the students to get to know her quickly. She was easy to love.

But even with the class's support, Olga was not immune to homesickness. Just before the Christmas holidays, she spoke of the traditions in her family, how she would miss the little things she'd taken for granted all of her life. The peer counselors were sensitive to her feelings and listened well.

Carmen said, "Listening to Olga makes me more aware of my own family, and I feel a new appreciation for tradition and expressions of love that I've never thought about before."

Olga was encouraged to talk to a peer counselor whenever she was feeling lonely. Not only did she share her feelings in class, but she also had the phone numbers of other students if she needed to call at night.

When spring came, Olga tried out for the lead in the senior play. This had been a dream of hers ever since she arrived. She had aspirations to be an actress, and playing the part of Anna in "The King and I" would be a step in that direction.

The class encouraged her. She heard, "Come on Olga, I know you can do it," "We believe in you," "Go for it," and "You'd be perfect."

I remember the day Olga found out she got the part. She was radiant. The class had received the news already by way of the grapevine, and jubilation abounded as Olga entered the room.

What a good choice Olga was to be in this role. Her performance as Anna gave her a standing ovation each night of the play.

In June, before she returned to Norway, she shared her feelings with the class.

''I've never received so much from a class as from this one. You have influenced my life—giving me encouragement to go on when I was homesick, helping build my self-esteem so that I had the confidence to try out for Anna, listening to my mixed feelings about being ready to go home to see my family but being sad about leaving my friends here. I hope you will always remember me as a girl who loved being a peer counselor and who loved all of you. I will never forget you.''

Olga was a winner!

Max, the rebel on campus, soon found out that he was accepted in class and there was no need for rebellion—at least, not for the one hour he was in peer counseling. Max was different though, as the students in the room realized from listening to his ''I feels.'' They were given the privilege of looking through the windows into the soul of a person they had never understood before. Why did Max risk his life by smoking pot, drinking beer, and then getting on that king-size motorcycle and racing home from parties? Why did he wear a chip on his shoulder that seemed to dare anyone to get too close? Why did he smoke on campus when he knew that eventually he'd get caught and be suspended?

The class learned how different his background was from most of theirs, and they soon realized why he saw things as he did. They didn't approve of his misbehavior—and he knew that—but they did approve of him as a worthwhile human being, and he soon had to accept that approval, even if it was difficult for him.

Caring about Max was also different and unusual for most students in the class. Heather wrote in her journal, "I worry about Max. Just saying that sounds strange to me because I have never known anyone like Max well enough to worry about. This time, I feel, worrying is positive though, not negative. I have grown, and my caring has been expanded. My arms now reach out farther to include people who I never even tried to understand before."

While Max didn't turn into a saint from others showing that they cared for him, he soon began to show signs of caring about himself. Later in the year he was able to reach even beyond himself and show concern for another person. I remember the day he spoke of his concern in class—.

"You, guys, gotta help me," he began. "Raymond, that no good cousin of mine, is really messing up. He was told today that he won't graduate unless he gets his act together—in a hurry."

"What's his problem?" Steve wanted to know.

"He will barely have enough credits to graduate as it is, and if he fails one class this semester, he's out. He's already nineteen and if he doesn't graduate, he won't come back next year. That will just about be it for him and his future. He will have failed again."

"What's happening this semester that's causing him to fail?" Faye asked.

"He's not coming to school enough because he's at the

beach half of the time. He's smart enough to pass if he'd just come, but he'll never pass civics if he's not in class. And if he doesn't pass civics, he won't graduate. Right now he has an "F" in civics and an "F" in English."

"Does he want help?" Jennifer asked.

"If he doesn't, he'd better." Max concluded. "Do you think someone in here could help him?"

The class seemed to sense that maybe helping Raymond was more important to do for Max than it was for Raymond—and they certainly wanted to help Max. They were quick to start brainstorming how they could help. Soon they arrived at a plan. Max would be responsible for talking to Raymond and helping him to see he had only nine weeks of school left to pull his grades up. If Max was successful—and Max felt the importance of his role in this—then stage two would go into effect.

Helen, Steve, Amy, and John would all meet with Raymond and discuss their plan. Helen would call Raymond every morning at 7 a.m. and Steve would go by his house at 7:45 to pick him up. Amy would tutor him in civics, and John would help him with English.

The plan sounded simple enough, but it would demand commitment on everyone's part. Nine weeks wasn't that long to catch up on all of the work Raymond needed to do, but it was a long time for Helen to remember to call every morning, and for Steve to sacrifice fifteen minutes of sleep each morning to go out of his way to pick Raymond up.

Max was successful—no one questioned how he did it—and the plan was put into action.

Each week for the next nine weeks, the class reviewed what had happened the previous week. One morning Raymond went back to sleep after Helen called. When Steve arrived and found Raymond still in bed, he simply went into his room, pulled him out of bed, wouldn't take no for answer, and got him to school on time, minus breakfast.

While I listened to Steve, I couldn't help but think, "These kids are able to accomplish something I would never be able to do as a counselor. Can you imagine how angry it would make a student if I attempted to do what these kids are doing? The influence they have over each other is nothing short of phenomenal. How refreshing to see that influence used in a positive way."

Amy tutored Raymond at least three times a week and arranged a once-a-week meeting with him and his civics teacher to chart his progress. One week Amy found out that Raymond had not turned in a report that was due the previous Friday. After that Amy got a list of forthcoming due dates from the teacher, and she made sure that Raymond didn't miss another one.

John reported that in helping Raymond, he realized how much he enjoyed English. Now he was seriously considering choosing it as a major in college and becoming an English teacher.

Everyone was interested in Raymond's progress, but no one more so than Max. He was the recognized leader of the project, and he watched over it like a mother hen. Having to be at school each day to check up on Raymond made Max's attendance so good that the attendance clerk wanted to know what had happened to him.

When graduation day came and Raymond's name was called, a loud sound of applause arose from one area of the audience. I couldn't see the faces as I sat on stage, but I knew that Max was in the middle of the group, enjoying his triumphant moment.

Max, the loser, had become a winner.

For the previous five or six years, the graduation exercises had gotten progressively more disruptive and noisy. After the behavior at last year's ceremony, the Board of Education had reached its limits and declared, "Enough is enough. This must change." Word was out to all of the teachers that the graduation ceremony would be stopped if it started to go in the disorderly direction it had gone the past year.

How sad it would be for the seniors if their graduation was terminated in the middle of the ceremony. To keep that from happening would require more than just the principal and teachers telling the students to behave themselves.

Why not use the peer counselors to get the word out to all of the various groups that everyone, including the seniors, wanted graduation to be different this year? If anyone could do it, the kids could. And Carmen, the senior class president, was an excellent peer counselor, concerned about others and energetic enough to get any job done. So why not let Carmen coordinate this undertaking? I brought the subject up for discussion approximately six weeks before graduation. I asked how the peer counselors, especially the ones who were seniors, felt about last year's graduation? How would they feel about having their graduation exercises cancelled during the ceremony? A lively discussion resulted. Some students thought a little fun was not harmful, but they understood that if there were to be graduation exercises this year, they must be conducted without disturbances.

Carmen took the lead in organizing the peer counselors. Each person would be responsible for spearheading certain segments of the student population. A campaign would be launched to get the seniors to take the initiative for making this graduation the best ever—one that following senior classes would want to live up to.

What a high expectation to put on a first-year peer counseling class. Carmen was a well-respected, strong leader, but would she be able to lead her classmates in this achievement?

On the day of graduation, the air was filled with excitement. As the seniors lined up in the gym before going onto the football field, I said a silent prayer that none of them was carrying a deflated beach ball, a firecracker, or a live mouse under his or her robe. I noticed Carmen circulating among some of the more mischievous students.

"Just checking," she said as she passed me to return to her place at the head of the line. "Everything is O.K., don't worry."

And she was right; everything was O.K. It was better than O.K. Graduation was flawless—not one firecracker or one beach ball, not even a tiny gray mouse.

True, the administration and the teachers had taken steps to improve the ceremony also. But the success of that graduation, and the example it set for other seniors to follow in the future, was due to the work of the kids, not us adults. It was particularly due to the work of one peer counselor, a senior class president named Carmen.

She was a winner.

Faye, Olga, Max, Carmen—all winners! And so were the other twenty-one students in that class. Each had his or her own victory, some measured in inches, not miles, but each was, nevertheless, a winner.

Crystal? Was she a winner too? Well, she didn't become

the most talkative girl in class, but she was able to develop trust in the other peer counselors and to share some of her deepest fears and frustrations. This was her victory.

Carmen wrote in her last journal, ''Being in this class has made me realize that the kids I viewed as losers were not losers at all. They just needed to find a peer who cared enough to look for the winner hiding somewhere in each of them.''

These peer counselors cared enough—.

CHAPTER SIX

Suicide—The Reality and the Support

"The metal box felt cold as I took it from the top of the chest. It was the size of a small shoe box. The day I'd brought it home from the mortuary was still vivid in my mind." Scott paused before continuing his story.

The peer counseling class sat listening in absolute silence. Many different life events had been shared during the semester, but this was more unusual than most.

Taking up where he left off Scott continued, "I carried the box almost reverently to the table where I had placed the brown wrapping paper, scissors, and mailing tape. There might be a law against mailing this box, but I wasn't concerned about it because no one would ever know what the package contained."

Scott—the recognized leader on campus, the jock, the

''A'' student, the student body officer—was revealing to the class a part of his life they would never have imagined possible. True, he had been in the class for less than a week, but most of the students felt they knew him before he entered their circle—at least, they knew of him. But what they were hearing now did not ''fit'' with their perceptions of this cheerful, outgoing boy.

He went on with his story. ''My brain was buzzing with plans as I folded the wrapping paper to meet on top of the box, tucked in the ends, and carefully pulled the sticky tape across the seams.

'''I must get grandmother's ashes to my aunt,' I thought as I wrapped that box for mailing. Suddenly an indescribable feeling of sadness came over me. After all, my grandmother had raised me. I was only six months old when my mother died in that terrible car accident.

''My father remarried six months later. He took my older brother with him. My two sisters were sent to my aunt's home. And my grandmother kept me. She was both a mother and a father to me for the next nine years because I seldom saw my father.

''I treasured that metal box I was holding in my hands. Even though I could never bring myself to open the box, I had always kept it near me. Now I had to give it away. I had to give away the possession that meant the most to me.''

John raised his hand and Scott acknowledged him, ''Before you joined our class, we studied about what behavior to look for in students who were thinking about suicide, and giving away their possessions was one of the characteristics. Did you know at the time that what you were doing was typical of a suicidal person?''

''No, I just knew what I planned to do, and I had to get

my grandmother's ashes to my aunt before I proceeded with my plan."

John nodded and Scott continued. "After mailing the package at the post office, I went immediately to the bank where I'd been working for the past year. I returned a book I'd borrowed to a co-worker. Then I left the watch I'd worn so proudly, after saving for months to buy it, at the teller station for Toby. He was the new employee I'd trained a few months previously. He admired the watch on more than one occasion, and I knew he'd treasure it as much as I did.

"Trish, the senior teller, joked with me as she counted out the money I was withdrawing, 'Must be some date you're going on tonight to take out all your savings.' Two hundred dollars wasn't a lot of money, but I'd worked hard to save that much as a cushion. Living on my own had made me aware that I would never know when an emergency might arise, and I'd need to have some money in reserve. I thought that if the savings were still there in May, I'd use it to go to the prom. Now I wouldn't need to worry about money for the prom."

Jill interrupted with, "Were you frightened at this point?"

"No, I was carrying out a well thought out plan, and going through the mechanics was like acting in a play that had already been rehearsed. The first thing I'd done that morning before getting my grandmother's ashes ready to mail, was to go to school, find a fellow class officer, and give him the key to the sound system. I knew the key would be needed for the noontime activities, and I delivered it before first period.

"Back to my story—. Leaving the bank, I went directly to a liquor store. With a fake I.D., I was able to buy some hard liquor. My next visit was to the drug store. This was my most important stop because I had to find two or three kinds of 'over-the-counter medicines' that would be the strongest I could take without a prescription. I read the labels on the boxes carefully, and then made my selections.

"I only had to wait a few minutes on the corner by the drug store before the city bus came along. The row of motels on the outskirts of town was only a few miles away, but this time I was in no mood to walk.

"The first two motels I came to had 'no vacancy' signs in front, but at the third one I was told a room was available on the second floor. I signed my name on the registry for room 206."

"Why were you going to do this at a motel instead of your own home?"asked Sandy.

"Because I no longer had my own home. In fact, I felt like I hadn't had my own home for the past year."

"What do you mean?" Sandy questioned.

"Maybe I should fill you in on a little of the background," Scott added.

Sandy nodded.

"My grandmother lived in New York, and I lived there with her until I was nine years old. At that time, my father decided to move to California. He took all of us, including my grandmother, with him. For the first time in my life I lived with my father. I found him to be a very abusive man, not to me, but to my older brother."

Questioningly Scott added, "You know, I've never been able to figure out why my brother has always loved and wanted to be near our father, and I've always disliked him and wanted to be as far away as possible. Yet it was my brother he mistreated, not me."

Steve added, "When I gave my report last semester on

child abuse, I found out that the abused child is usually very protective of his abuser. The child often feels that it's his fault and that somehow he's responsible for the treatment he receives. Maybe those same feelings applied to your brother."

Scott nodded and then continued his story. "When I was eleven, my father married for the fourth time. Grandmother went back to New York, and my brother and I were alone with my father and his new wife. Those were not the best years of my life, but I survived them partly due to the fact that my step-mother was a person I could relate to. She treated me well.

"When I was thirteen, I went to New York and spent a month with my grandmother. When I returned my father had moved out, and I stayed with my stepmother for the next six months—which was great. But then my father came and took me to his apartment.

"The next few months, I learned more about my father than I really wanted to know. I found out that he was a drug dealer and heavily involved with a large group of very unsavory characters.

"Life was not pleasant. At times, he would lock me out of the apartment; other times, he would completely ignore me for weeks. One night, he became violent, and I ran away for a week. Things went from bad to worse, and I finally ended up moving to my aunt's house here.

"That's when you enrolled at our junior high school," Amy injected.

"Yes, I came here in seventh grade and I lived with my aunt until the tenth grade. Things went well for those first three years, but my older brother moved in and things began to fall apart. Fortunately, a family in the community invited me to live with them, and I moved in.

"To answer your question, why I didn't do it at home, the answer would be that I didn't want to cause the family I was living with any grief. They had three adopted children, and their oldest son had tried to commit suicide. I didn't want to put them through it again."

"You left us on a real cliff hanger," Sue said. "Could you tell us what happened at the motel?"

"Of course, I just wanted to give you a little background first.

"When I entered the motel room, I noticed how dark the room was. The carpet and bedspread were a very dark olive green, and the lined drapes kept the sunlight from coming through the windows.

"Without turning on the light, I walked to the television and turned on a rerun of one of my favorite programs. I began to drink the liquor, as I sat down and thought about my life.

"There were many questions for which I didn't have the answers: Why had my life not worked out as I wanted it to? Why did my mother die when I was so young? My father had been in the same car accident, but he had walked away without a scratch. Why did the drunk who was driving the other car kill my mother? Why didn't I have a normal family life like the one I saw in the home where I was staying?"

"How are you defining normal?" Sue asked.

"For the first time in my life, I saw a mother, father and three kids functioning in a home as a family—a family sitting down at a dinner table and each member sharing the events of the day with the others. I saw what I'd missed all of my life. And the irony of it was that each of the three kids in that home was adopted. At sometime in their life they'd been at the same place I'd been— without a family. But they'd been chosen to receive the benefits of an adopted mother and father who loved them, a beautiful home to live in, nice clothes, a car, and money to go to college. I hadn't had any of those things; and the fact that my peers were applying to top-ranked colleges, and I wasn't, really hit hard. It wouldn't have been so bad if I hadn't earned the grades to get in, but I had. I'd worked hard and all during my tenth and eleventh grade years, I had straight 'A's' on my report card.

''I had all of the things that the top universities look for in students—grades, leadership in extracurricular activities, high SAT scores, good recommendations about my character, initiative, creativity, motivation. I had it all—except the money— and I thought that was a good enough reason not to apply. I'd have to settle for going to the local community college and working at the bank. I didn't know where I'd live because the family I was presently staying with was moving in a month to another city.

''You sound as if you were very depressed.'' Steve added.

''I was very depressed.''

''No one noticed?'' Steve asked.

''No, because when I was around people, I played the role of being my same old 'up-self'. I was a fun guy, and I continued to play the role.''

As I listened to Scott talk, I thought of the many other times I had heard students use the phase, ''I played the role.'' What a coping mechanism that had become for teenagers. The ''let's pretend'' of the young child seemed to easily carry over in a more sophisticated way to the teenage years. If only parents and teachers could see beyond the roles that are played each day, how much more effective they could be in really understanding the young person.

Scott continued, "I'd been depressed since the beginning of my senior year. This was the year my friends were enjoying— they were excited about their future—but I was afraid of mine."

"You were in the motel, drinking liquor and watching a television show. What happened next?" Sue questioned.

"After I had a few drinks, I started taking the pills. I took uppers, and downers, and a wide assortment of pills."

"Can you describe your thoughts during this time?" Betty wanted to know.

"Soon, I began to feel terrible pains in my chest, stomach, arms, and legs. I was perspiring profusely. God, was I sick. I kept thinking, 'Why don't I die?'

"Another few minutes passed—my head was still pounding, and my heart felt like it would jump out of my chest. I didn't know how much more of that pain I could take.

"Thoughts began to enter my brain, such as, 'Is this worth it? Do I really have that many problems? Will things get better if I survive this?'

"Mainly I began to think, 'Why am I dying?'

"My heart was beating at double speed, pounding in my chest like the ocean pounding against a seawall. My stomach burned like a hot iron had been placed in the center with all sides touching the iron. A sledge hammer was hitting the top of my head, driven by a three-hundred pound man. The pain I was feeling was sheer hell—dying wasn't supposed to be like this.

"Why didn't I die? I was trying so hard. I kept telling myself, 'Come on die—die.'

"Maybe the struggle to die made me realize that if I could

fight to die, I could also fight to live.

"I rolled over on my side and flung my hand out toward the night stand. That phone had to be there. The room was dark, the only light was coming from the television screen.

"Squinting to focus my eyes, I saw the telephone through my blurred vision. I reached again; this time I made contact with the receiver.

"The motel desk clerk's voice came on the phone, and I said, 'Get me an ambulance; I tried to kill myself.'

"The person on the desk seemed to know just what to do. He told me to keep talking while he called the ambulance on another line. In the short time it took for the ambulance to get there, the desk clerk kept me talking continually. When the paramedic van arrived, he had a key ready for them to get into my room.

"The paramedics worked very quickly and had me at the hospital in a matter of minutes. I remember slipping in and out of consciousness, and one time when I heard the beep of the monitoring machine, I remember thinking, 'I'm still alive.'

"As the doctors in the emergency room were working over me, I remember hearing one of them say, 'Kid, you're a fighter. Don't give up now. Nothing can be that bad. Life has to be better than death. Come on, Kid, fight.'

"And I guess I did just that."

The class sat for a few minutes before they responded. Then Sue said, "Life is better, Scott, and we want to show you how much better it can be. I, too, felt life was pretty crummy at one time. Now that I'm no longer on drugs, I can see how special just living each day can be."

Scott nodded. "I stayed in the hospital for a couple of days, and on my first day back to school, Tom grabbed me by the arm and said, 'Hey, Man, I heard what you tried to do. You need to be in my peer counseling class where you can talk about your feelings.'

"So here I am. I guess I do need support. The therapist who was assigned to my case at the hospital wants to continue seeing me once a week and he suggested I get into this class. He said that he'd been in this class as a guest speaker, and he really liked the support system he saw among you people."

Sue and Scott became very good friends. He did receive the support that the therapist, Mr. Miles, had talked about. Mr. Miles must have been pleased with the progress Scott made from week to week because he continued to suggest to his high school patients that they either get enrolled in peer counseling, or, if that was not possible because the class was full, that they ask for a peer counselor to be assigned to them. Not only did the peer counselors support Mr. Miles' high school patients, but Mr. Miles supported our peer counseling program. He took time to visit our class and discuss the many aspects of the suicidal person and to answer questions about problems other than suicide. He "role played" with the students to instruct them on how important it is to take every threat or sign of suicide seriously and how very imperative it is to get help quickly when a student begins to hint about it.

The peer counselor does not counsel the student who is threatening suicide. He knows that confidentiality is no longer required and that he must get help for that student. After the student's parents have been made aware of the situation and he or she is receiving professional help, then the peer counselor is available to support and listen—and to be aware so he can alert someone if the student begins to talk about attempting suicide a second time.

Sometimes one of the students in the peer counseling class begins dropping hints of suicide in his or her "I feel" sessions. Tray was one of those students.

"I really think life sucks," Tray began. "My parents are always fighting; my school work is going down hill—fast; I get stomach aches nearly every day. I sometimes think it would be easier just to end it all."

"What do you mean 'end it all'?" Rachael asked.

The tall, good-looking sophomore thought for a moment and then said, "I mean it would be easier to just die and not have to get up in the morning and face another miserable day."

As he completed his sentence, the bell sounded and I told him I would like to explore the subject further with him. He did not object to my request and we proceeded to my office.

"Are you thinking of killing yourself?" I asked straightforwardly.

"Yes, I've been thinking about it for several weeks now. There just doesn't seem to be another way out. I hate school now because I'm behind with my work and can't seem to catch up. I guess I really don't try any more because I'm always tired and sleepy in class."

"You're tired and sleepy in class," I restated his comment.

"Yes, I can't sleep at night at my house. My dad works the evening shift, and he doesn't get home until after eleven o'clock. That's when the fighting begins. My room is next to my parents' and the walls are like cardboard. I can hear everything they say when they speak in a normal tone, so you can imagine how loud it is when they're yelling and screaming at each other until two or three every morning.

By the time the yelling stops, I'm usually so tense I can't go to sleep for another hour or two. Sometimes I wish they would get divorced so one of them would move out and I could get some sleep."

"Have you talked to your parents about being unable to sleep?"

"We don't really talk at my house. I've tried talking to my mom, but she doesn't get home until six or seven—sometimes even later now. Ever since the store she works for started having financial troubles, she's been staying late to help get the place straightened out. If things don't get better she may lose her job, and she's very fearful of that happening. A lot of the fights she has with my dad have to do with money problems."

"You mentioned in class you're having stomach aches daily."

"That's my ulcer acting up."

"You've seen a doctor?"

"I've been seeing doctors off and on for the past four years. The stomach aches started when I entered junior high. They go away for a few months, sometimes longer after I've taken the medicine for a while, and then they come back. I get sick and tired of always feeling bad. It's just a 'pain in the neck'."

I restated what I'd heard, "Family life isn't good right now, school is a drag, you aren't feeling well and you've about decided life isn't worth the effort."

"That sums it up. Yep, that's just the way it is."

"Do you have a plan as to how you are going to kill yourself?" I asked this question because we know that students who have a plan are more serious about carrying out their threats than those who haven't thought about these steps.

"Not exactly, but I know I'd use a gun."

"Do you have a gun?"

"No, but my dad does, and I know where he keeps it."

Only two weeks previously, Mr. Miles had told the class that more girls attempt suicide than boys, but more boys are successful than girls. Boys tend to use guns or more violent weapons than girls do, and that eliminates the chance for having second thoughts, as is sometimes the case after taking pills.

"Tray, you remember when I told you at the beginning of the semester that I would break confidentiality if I felt a student's life was in jeopardy. I believe what you have told me this morning, and I care too much about you not to try to get help for you. I'm going to call your mother and ask her to come to my office, and I want you to tell her exactly what you have told me."

Tray did not protest. In fact, he seemed relieved that he would be able to talk to his mother in a school setting.

After he had repeated his story to his mother, she stated, "This does it. Something has to be done. Oftentimes I feel the same way Tray does. In fact, if it weren't for the responsibility I feel for Tray, I would have left his dad a long time ago. Life has just gotten out of hand for all three of us. We all need help."

We discussed the possibility of getting family counseling with an agency that has a sliding pay scale. Tray's mother said that she thought her insurance covered family counseling and that she would check into it immediately.

The next day she called to tell me her insurance did cover a certain number of visits and she had already make an appointment for herself and Tray. She was hoping to get her husband to go with them some time in the near future.

Not all families see a need for counseling as quickly as this one did; but fortunately for Tray, his family wanted help. All three attended weekly meetings, and Tray shared in "I feel" sessions how helpful going to these group meetings was for the entire family.

The peer counselors helped Tray catch up with his school work, and with the stomach aches gradually subsiding, there was no further problem with missing classes and getting behind. Tray reported that his parents had drawn up a contract to discuss only noncontroversial things after 11 p.m. Since they weren't fighting, he was no longer finding it difficult to sleep.

Peer counselors do not take talk about suicide lightly, nor does the teacher. Fortunately there is a class like this on campus where students can share their feelings—even those dark feelings of death. As long as they can talk about them, then maybe there is hope for finding help for these kids.

Scott, Tray, and many others have found help. At the time of this writing (four years after peer counseling was introduced on our campus) there has not been one suicide among the high school students.

By May, Scott had managed to get the money together to go to that prom he'd been thinking about earlier in the year. As I sat at the table near the dance floor, I enjoyed seeing the girls in their beautiful dresses and the boys standing tall in their tuxedos. But I especially took note of Scott and Sue. They were both good dancers—not missing a beat as they laughed and talked while keeping time with the music—and without question having a good time. I couldn't help but think, "Thank God, Scott is alive to enjoy this night."

CHAPTER SEVEN
Dreams—They Do Come True

"What do you mean, we don't have any money?" Lucas asked with disbelief in his voice. "Mr. Briggs told us weeks ago that the school district would provide money for the conference."

"You're right. That's what Mr. Briggs said," I assured Lucas. "But principals are allowed a mistake once in a while too. Apparently there was a mix-up. I don't quite understand it myself, but when I sent in the written request for 140 students to attend the conference, Mr. Briggs said it was turned down at the district level."

"Are you telling us that with only two weeks before the conference, now we don't have any money?" Betty asked.

"I'm afraid so." I replied.

"But we've looked forward to this for months. We've followed the planning for this very first California Peer Counseling Association Conference from stage one. I don't even want to think about not going,'' Sue said in a non-accepting voice.

''I didn't say anything about not going,'' I said calmly.

''But if we don't have any money and the registration fee is twenty dollars per student, how are we going to get in?'' Sue probed.

''Mrs. Sturkie can sneak us in the back door,'' Jeff said with a twinkle in his eye.

''That would take some doing to sneak in 140 people,'' I replied with a chuckle. ''Maybe we'd better come up with a better idea.''

''What about buses? Are they going to pay for buses?'' Steve asked.

''That was not approved either,'' I reluctantly confessed. ''The school district seems to be very low in field trip funds right now.''

''Two weeks before the conference, and we have no money and no buses,'' Paul emphasized his statement by raising his arms and then dropping them to his side.

''But we do have two weeks,'' I said. ''True, it would have been better if we'd known about this a month or two ago, but we didn't. We all believed everything was taken care of. Now we have a decision to make.''

''Luckily, we've already completed our unit on 'Decision Making,' '' Nancy said jokingly.

''That's right,'' Lucas injected. ''And our decision will be made based on the values of the class.''

''I'm impressed, Lucas,'' I teased. ''You do remember that unit.''

''First, let's identify the problem,'' Sally said.

''That's an easy one,'' Betty jumped to answer. ''No

money, no buses—and five classes of peer counselors who want to go to the state peer counseling conference."

"Let's brainstorm alternatives," Emily suggested.

"O.K." Steve began. "We can accept what has happened to us this year and start raising funds months in advance for next year's conference."

"That's a lousy idea," Lucas said quickly. "Sorry, Steve, I didn't mean that as a put-down. I'm just thinking that, for seniors, there is no next year. Either we go this year or we don't go."

"Lucas is right," Melanie defended. "I'm a senior, and I want to go this year."

"But we don't have any money," Steve said logically.

"Why can't we get it?" Melanie responded.

"Let's see," Jeff said, already punching the small calculator he'd taken from his pocket. "With 140 of us going, that would come to $2800.00."

"Twenty-eight hundred dollars," Betty seemed to hang on to each word. "We could take a trip to the moon about as easy as we could raise that kind of money."

"Well, we'll never know until we've tried." Peter said optimistically.

I contributed, "From what I seem to be hearing, some of you want to try to raise the money and others would rather wait and work on it for next year. Are there any other alternatives you want to discuss?"

I waited for a moment, and when no one responded, I asked, "Is there any further discussion on the two alternatives?"

Jill raised her hand. I nodded and she began speaking, "We know decisions are based on values, and I think we need to focus on what we value. At least, I'd like to tell you what I value.''

After a pause, she continued. ''I value our class and our peer counseling program. I value going to the conference and meeting other students and sharing ideas. I feel that it will be very helpful to hear the speakers and attend the workshops. I guess what I'm trying to say is that I value this conference, and I'm willing to work hard to raise the money.''

''Right on,'' Melanie cheered. ''Count me in.''

''Me, too,'' said Steve.

''And me,'' volunteered Amy.

''Let's go for it,'' Lucas encouraged.

There was an excited buzz around the room. I felt that an informal vote had already been taken, but I wanted this to be a unanimous decision because I knew each person would need to make an all-out effort if we were to be successful.

''If you're ready to make your decision, I'd like to call for the vote,'' I said. ''How many of you would like to postpone the trip until next year?''

Not a hand went up.

''How many would like to try to raise the money to go this year?''

A cheer went up and every person in the room raised a hand—some raised two.

''You have just voted to put yourself to work. This will take an effort on everyone's part. However, before we can begin, we must get votes from the other four classes. I'll talk to them today and report back to you tomorrow.''

I had little doubt as to how the other classes would vote, and I was right. They overwhelmingly voted to raise money.

The next day we took a few minutes at the beginning of the class to decide what type of fund raisers we'd have.

''Whatever we do, we must do it quickly because now we are down to 13 days,'' Jill said.

''Melanie, would you write the suggestions on the chalk board?'' I asked.

John began, ''We have already planned a shirting banquet for next week. Why don't we ask for donations at the door?''

''That's a good idea, John,'' Lucas complimented. ''The parents, administrators, and other guests are getting a free dinner because we're providing a potluck meal; therefore, it doesn't seem like too much to ask for a small donation.''

The shirting banquet they were referring to is held twice a year, after each beginning peer counseling class has completed its first semester. Taken from the idea of student nurses receiving their ''capping'' when they are ready to begin working on a hospital floor, the peer counselors receive their ''shirting'' when they are prepared to go out on campus and function as peer counselors. For the entire first semester, while they are developing their skills, they are not allowed to counsel students on campus.

At the banquet, peer counselors speak first and later parents and other guests join in with their own ''I feel.'' Parents seem to enjoy expressing their feelings and sharing how their lives have been affected by having a son or daughter take peer counseling. Hearing positive reports from parents is inspirational for all of us.

I also have the class do the ''self-esteem card'' on the day before the banquet. This exercise consists of giving each student a 5x7 white card and asking each one to write his or her name at the very top. The card is then passed to the right. If the person sitting in that seat wants to write a one line, positive sentence about the person whose name appears at the top, he does that. He then passes it on to his right. If he does not want to write anything, he just passes it on.The only rule is that whatever is written on the card must be positive and must be sincere.

After a card has been passed all around the circle, I collect it before it reaches the person whose name appears at the top. I then shuffle the cards, and pass them out again, making sure no one receives his or her own card. The students then read the card they are holding, and the class guesses who the student is. Some of the comments are real self-esteem builders. They include ''you're terrific,'' ''beautiful eyes,'' ''sensitive and caring,'' ''great smile,'' ''love your accent,'' ''good listener.''

Then at the banquet, as each student is coming forward to receive the sweatshirt with the peer counseling monogram across the front, a portion of his or her card is read by a fellow student.

The shirting ceremony is always a very special time for everyone.

Students representing each advanced class attend also to show their support for the newly designated peer counselors.

Now Lucas was asking a question that brought my thoughts back to the present problem at hand. ''How about getting a few merchants to donate gifts we could give out at the banquet? We could sell tickets and have a drawing.''

''I'd like to help with that,'' Gina volunteered.

''Jack and I will help too,'' Penny said.

''We will?'' Jack questioned with a smile coming over his face.

''We will,'' Penny affirmed. Lately, I'd noticed that Penny and Jack were arriving and leaving the class together.

"I have heard two suggestions, both to take place at the banquet. Do I hear any others?" I asked.

"We need something that will bring in a lot of money, quickly," Lucas emphasized.

"Such as?" Steve questioned.

Lucas began to divulge his plan, "I think we should print a flyer telling about our peer counseling program, how helpful it has been to all of us, and how much we'd like to attend the conference."

"Who would we give these flyers to?" Melanie asked.

"We would take a map and divide the city into sections. Each person would take a section and hand-carry a flyer to the merchants and businesses in that section."

"That sounds like a wonderful idea," Penny said excitedly. "We could wear our peer counseling shirts and talk to each manager or owner in person when we drop off the flyers."

"Sounds great. I'm sure businesses would like to help if they knew how much it means to us," Melanie said.

After two or three more students had talked about the merits of this type of fund raiser I spoke, "There are several positive sides to this suggestion. Number one, you may raise some money."

"Right on, Mrs. Sturkie. I like that," Lucas jested.

"And," I continued after smiling and nodding to Lucas, "you may create some good PR for our program. I'm sure some people are not aware what peer counseling is. I hope you will take the time to explain the program and answer questions."

"I'm afraid I'm not very good at asking strangers for money," Jack injected. "You don't need to ask for money," Melanie replied. "Just talk about our program and how going to the conference will help us. I think we should leave the flyer one day and tell them we will be back the next day to answer any questions, after they've had time to read what we've left them. We could also pick up the donation on the second visit. That would give them time to think about it and write out their checks.''

''Maybe they will make their checks for a larger amount if they're given time to think about it overnight,'' Steve added.

I said, ''I want us to talk about how you will approach these people and how you will handle an acceptance of a donation—or a rejection. Sometimes it's easy to take a rejection personally, and I don't want any of you feeling you've failed if someone turns you down. Remember the person is not rejecting you as a person; he's rejecting the idea of giving money.''

''You're trying to prepare us for coming back empty-handed?'' Lucas joked.

''I want you to be prepared for the fact that not all the businesses in town will be eagerly awaiting your visit. Some may be as short on funds as we are. However, you can turn the visit into a worthwhile experience by letting them see teenagers in a positive light—trying to help each other.''

''Sounds good. Let's go for it,'' Steve said eagerly.

For the next few minutes the class discussed who would be in charge of designing the brochure, who would divide the map into sections and what dates would be best for carrying out their project after school hours.

''We still need some more fund-raising ideas,'' Melanie added after the class had finished their discussion. ''Remember $2800.00 is a lot of money.''

''How about asking our own parents for donations?''

Betty suggested. "My dad's an accountant, and he said if the checks are made out to the California Peer Counseling Association, the donation will be tax deductible. Of course, the money will go into the general fund, not meant for just one particular student to go. Also, some of our parents may work at businesses outside the city, and their companies may be willing to donate."

"That's a good idea, Betty," Jack said.

"Some of us have part-time jobs, and maybe we will be able to donate a small amount," Jill added.

"Are you kidding!" injected Steve. "My car takes every cent I make."

"I can relate to that myself," Jill responded, "but I don't think everyone who works is as broke as you and I are."

For the next few days there was a furor of activity before and after school, at lunch—any time the students had a few minutes to get together and work on their project.

In a few days, checks slowly began coming in. Most were donations from the parents of the peer counselors.

Then came the shirting banquet. Excitement filled the air that night as parents, school board members, administrators, and teachers began to fill the school cafeteria.What a surprise to see the usually large, drab room, come alive with bright colored balloons floating from the centerpieces on each table.The black and white checked table clothes and the black and orange crepe paper streamers, draping the tops and sides of the windows, accented the school colors.

Each class receiving sweatshirts had been allowed to vote on the colors for the shirt and the lettering. There were three different stacks of shirts on the tables behind the podium, reflecting the votes of the three classes. The shirts in the stack on the left were royal blue with white lettering; the middle ones were bright red with white lettering; and the ones on the right were dark blue with a light blue lettering. The make-up of the class was as different as the shirt colors they had chosen, but the purpose of helping their peers was the same.

The gifts for the drawing had been arranged with local businesses—a dinner for two at a restaurant, a clock, a flower arrangement, golf balls, and a variety of other gifts.Tickets had been sold for the drawing. A total of $200.00 had been collected, and donations at the door that evening brought in another $260.00.

One week before the conference, a total of $1200.00 had been collected.

''We need $1600.00 more before we'll have enough, and where are we going to get that much?'' Melanie asked, her voice revealing a hint of despair.

''Are we sure we've covered all the sections of town?'' asked Steve.

''I covered mine,'' said Kyle, ''but most of them asked me to just leave the material. They said they would send in the check if they decided to make a donation.''

''The same goes here,'' verified Sue.

''I have collected some,'' began Amy, ''but mostly only ten or twenty dollar checks. It takes so many of them for the kind of money we need.''

''Well, let's just keep working,'' Helen encouraged. ''My mother works at a bank, and the manager told her the bank will donate a hundred dollars. We should receive that soon.''

After school was out that same afternoon, I was working in my office when Kyle appeared at my open door unannounced—and breathless. He began speaking a mile a minute before I could even acknowledge his presence.

''We have just been given a thousand dollar donation,''

the words spilled from his mouth.

"He'd make a good actor," I thought as I noted his convincing expression and voice tone. I could almost believe him myself.

"Kyle, I appreciate your humor, but I've had a long day."

"I'm not kidding you, Mrs. Sturkie. A woman has just given us a check for one thousand dollars."

"O.K., Kyle, if you say so. How about letting me see the check?" I said, going along with his game.

"She said her secretary would get it ready, and I could pick it up tomorrow."

"Kyle, come on now. You can't expect me to believe that."

With a twinkle in his eye and obviously enjoying himself, he said, "But it's true. Honest, I swear, it's true."

I was becoming more interested, but still very cautious. "Sit down, Kyle, and let's hear your story."

"Several days ago, I went to a commercial development company. I just happened to notice it in a small office building across the street from Marty's Qwick Stop—you know, the one down on Center Street."

"I know Marty's Qwick Stop, but I've never noticed an office building across from it. But do go on."

"I don't know why I decided to walk across the street, but I did. When I went into the office the secretary told me that the owner, Mrs. Snyder, was on the phone, but I could wait. Very soon this nice-looking woman appeared and asked what she could do for me. I told her about our peer counseling program and about the conference. She asked me to leave her some literature, but I didn't have any with me. I told her I'd drop a pamphlet off the following day."

"Then you went back the next day?" I asked.

"Yes, but when I gave her the pamphlet, she asked me to come back in a few days, to give her a chance to read it."

Kyle continued, "I went back today, and she said she liked what she'd read."

"'How much does your group need to go to this conference?' she asked me. And I said, 'About a thousand dollars more than we have.'

"She replied, 'I'll donate a thousand dollars—my secretary will get it ready, and you can pick it up tomorrow.'"

"Kyle, as much as I'd like to believe a thousand dollars will arrive tomorrow, I'm afraid that I can't. You must have misunderstood—or maybe she was just joking with you."

"Here's her card," Kyle said as he reached in his pocket and produced a business card. "Why don't you call her?"

As I looked at the card, I noticed that it read exactly as Kyle had related it to me—K. Snyder Company, Commercial Developers.

I reached for the phone and said to Kyle as I dialed, "I'm going to feel very foolish to this woman says she doesn't know what I'm talking about."

The secretary answered and asked me to please wait. Momentarily, a friendly voice greeted me, "This is K. Snyder. May I help you?"

I identified myself and then said, "I have a young man sitting in my office who seems to think that you are donating a thousand dollars for our peer counselors to go to the state conference."

Before I could continue, she interrupted, "That's true. I plan to give a thousand dollars to the California Peer Counseling Association to contribute toward your students going to the conference."

"How wonderful!" I managed to exclaim as I looked at

Kyle.

He was nodding and smiling as if to say, "I told you so."

I continued, "This will mean so much to our peer counselors. We all sincerely appreciate what you're doing."

"I'm very impressed with that young man who visited my office—he followed through extremely well. I am also equally impressed with your peer counseling program. I just wish there had been a class like this when I was in school."

"I hope you'll visit our class. We'd like very much to have you see our program first hand."

"Thank you for the invitation. I'd like to do that."

After I said good-bye and placed the phone down, I turned to Kyle and screamed, "Y-e-a-h!"

Hugging him I said, "I'm so proud of you, Kyle. What a difference this thousand dollars will make."

Kyle picked the check up the following day, and it did make the difference—all the difference in the world. Now only $600.00 was needed instead of $1600.00. The goal was reachable, and the check provided the extra motivation to double the efforts to raise the remaining money.

Three days before the conference, I sent in all of the money to the California Peer Counseling Association, and the reservations were secured.

On the day of the First Annual Peer Counseling Conference, 133 kids (seven were ill and unable to attend) piled into cars and vans driven by parents and students. They journeyed to the conference and joined other peer counselors from all over the state to bring the total attendance to 670 people. Our kids represented the largest group from any one school—and they were there because they had raised every cent of the money themselves.

As president of the newly formed California Peer Counseling Association, I stood up to welcome the standing-room-only crowd congregated in the ballroom of that large hotel.

I began my greeting by saying, "I hope all of you believe that your dream can come true because today mine has. I dreamed that peer counselors would be able to meet together, share ideas, make friends, hear noted speakers, acquire knowledge, and return to their schools to be better peer counselors. I first dreamed that dream two years ago, and I called peer counseling teachers from three other schools and invited them to meet at my school and talk about such a conference. As a result of that initial meeting and subsequent ones, the California Peer Counseling Association was formed and this conference was planned. Dreams do come true."

At noon, Lucas, Melanie, and Betty passed me in the hall on their way from a workshop to the dining room.

"Hey, Mrs. Sturkie, isn't this great!" Lucas exclaimed.

"Couldn't be better," I responded.

After they had passed me, Melanie called back over her shoulder, "And to think, two weeks ago we had no money and no buses. Dreams do come true, Mrs. Sturkie."

Yes, they surely do.

CHAPTER EIGHT

Incest—The Hidden Secret

Looking around the class, Dr. Rice remarked, "In a group this size, some studies would indicate that at least five of you have been victims of sexual abuse. Most of which was incestuous."

There was complete silence in the room, with all eyes staring straight ahead at Dr. Rice. I had the feeling that the students didn't want to look at each other in fear of seeing an expression on someone's face that would verify what Dr. Rice had just said. Being unaware was safer.

The class listened as the guest speaker for the day continued, "Incest is much more common than was thought in the past. It may have always been all too common, but more cases are being reported now. Unfortunately, the number of unreported cases are probably equal, if not more, than the reported ones."

Stephanie raised her hand, "I don't understand why so many cases go unreported."

Dr. Rice answered, ''It is very difficult for victims to report a family member who lives with them. Oftentimes the abused person feels that no one will believe him or her, and some times no one does. Other times, the victims are afraid the abusing adult will be removed from the home and their financial support will be cut off. These are just a few of the reasons that crimes committed in the home go unreported.''

''How can we help?'' Gary asked.

''As peer counselors, you may have an opportunity to help some of these victims. And if you do, you will be able to fill a void that often goes unfilled. When elementary aged children and junior and senior high kids are abused, they find themselves with a secret they're afraid to share. I hope with your training in listening skills and your availability on a daily basis, you will be able to reach them and get help. You are less threatening to talk with than most of us adults in the helping professions.''

As Dr. Rice spoke, I looked around the room. I felt I knew these students pretty well, but since they were only in the second quarter of their beginning semester, I didn't know them as well as I knew the advanced classes. But even knowing students very well did not mean that they would share something as frightening as incest.

Dr. Rice had everyone's undivided attention. Maybe the statistics did not hold up for this class. Maybe no one in the class was a victim of incest.

These unrealistic thoughts crumbled the very next day. As I stood at the door greeting the students, Sonja stopped at the threshold. Placing her clammy hand on my arm, she said, ''I know today isn't an 'I feel' day, but I've got to talk to the class. May I please have a few minutes at the beginning of the period?''

Looking at Sonja, I saw an attractive young girl dressed in jeans, a bright red and blue plaid shirt, and a blue sweater tied around her shoulders. Yesterday she had looked like a typical high school sophomore, but today there was something different about her. Was it the red-streaked, swollen eyes, the look of anxiousness, or the pleading sound of her voice? Whatever it was, I felt that what she had to say was too important to delay.

I said, "Of course, Sonja, you may speak immediately after roll call. We will postpone the lesson until later."

Somehow, I knew then that the lesson I'd stayed up late the previous night preparing wouldn't be presented today. But the lesson could wait. Sonja's need could not.

After a brief explanation to the class, I turned to Sonja and said, "Go right ahead."

For a moment I thought she was going to tell us that she'd changed her mind. She hesitated and looked around the room with a frightened glance, almost like she was searching for something or someone.

Mandy seemed to sense this too and said, "We're here for you, Sonja."

"I know," Sonja responded, "But I've never told anyone what I'm about to tell you—and it's hard to start."

"Take your time, Sonja," Bill said. "You don't need to hurry."

The sensitivity of the students made me wonder if they suspected that Sonja's story would relate to the topic of yesterday's guest speaker.

"Two days ago I had no idea I'd be telling you this today," Sonja began, "but after I listened to Dr. Rice yesterday, I knew that I wasn't alone—that there are hundreds more like me. Somehow, I felt more secure when I learned there were so many. At least, I'm not some kind of a freak."

"I don't know what you have to tell us," Fred emphasized, "but whatever it is, I can assure you, you're no freak."

Encouraged, Sonja continued, "I am one of the people Dr. Rice was talking about yesterday—one of the unreported cases."

"Oh, God!" Lynn let slip under her breath.

Hearing her, Sonja responded, "I know, you would never have known, would you? It's just like Dr. Rice said. No one suspects because most of us never talk about it. If it wasn't for this class, I'd continue to live with this nightmare all alone. I know I could never reach for the phone and report my own father, but I know he needs help. And he will only get that help if someone knows what he is doing, and he gets psychological counseling. But I can't report him myself. I know I should, but I just can't. He's my father, and I love him."

Jenny spoke up this time, "You know by talking about this in class, Mrs. Sturkie will have to file a report?"

"That's what I thought about all last night—whether I should talk about it, knowing it will have to be reported, or whether I should keep quiet and continue to live in the hell I've been living in.

"About 6 a.m., I made my decision. At that time I heard my father's alarm go off. I heard him leave his bedroom and start walking down the hallway toward my room. I quickly jumped out of bed, crossed the floor to my bathroom, closed the door and turned on the shower. I was leaning against the door in the bathroom when I heard my bedroom door open and then close again. If I hadn't been awake when my father's alarm went off, he would have found me in bed and crawled in with me.

"While I was leaning against the bathroom door, with the water running full force in the shower, I made my decision. I could not continue to live like this. I think I realized that I'd rather kill myself than continue to live in this fear—fear that someone would find out, and at the same time, fear that no one would."

"Would you like to talk about this in private or to the entire class?" I asked.

"I'd like for the entire class to hear my story so that if there are other people in this class who have the same problem, then maybe they will know they're not alone."

"It's up to you," I said. "If you wish to, why don't you start at the beginning."

"This all started when I was about seven years old, which was about eight years ago." She stopped and then seemed to ask herself, 'How could this have gone on for eight years?' I don't know, but it did.

"Eight years ago, my father was very successful in his career, but then things seemed to start going badly for him, and my mother had to go to work. My father was home for long periods of time, and it was during this time he started assuming most of the household chores, including looking after my younger brother and me.

"One night when I got ready for my bath, he said, "Wait a minute and I'll take a bath with you. I'm tired and you can scrub my back."

"I washed his back, and he washed mine, and taking a bath was fun. I liked my father's attention. I had him all alone without having to share him with my younger brother.

"We continued to take baths together, and soon we were washing each other's face, arms, legs. When he first started washing 'all of me,' I felt uneasy, like—this isn't right. But then I'd remember that he was my father, and I knew he wouldn't do anything that was wrong. My mother knew about the baths, and she didn't say anything—so it must be all right.

"Then my father asked me to wash 'all of him.' I didn't want to, but I wanted to please my father—so I did.

"I'd always been 'daddy's little girl.' From the time I started to walk, he showed me off to all of his friends and told them I was his little princess. He bragged about me all the time, and displayed me like I was a doll. Buying me gifts was a weekly occasion, and whatever he couldn't afford, he'd promise me that someday he would have the money to get it for me.

"When I look back now, I can see why my brother, who is three years younger than I am, became such a little monster. He wanted and deserved some attention from our father, but he never got any. Father gave all of his attention to me."

"What about your mother?" Jim asked. "Were you close to your mother?"

"My mother was working all of the time—at least, it seemed that way to me. She began to be very successful on her job, and the more successful she became, the longer hours she worked. Soon she'd turned over all the child-rearing duties to my father.

"Before long, father was crawling in bed with me at night 'to cuddle as he read to me.'

"I knew something was wrong, but I knew that my father loved me. He would never do anything to intentionally hurt me.

"I was becoming more and more confused, and there was no one to talk to. I was afraid to tell my mother because first of all, she wouldn't believe me and second of all, I felt like it was my fault."

"Did you think your dad was different from other dads?" Jane asked.

"That's the strange part. All of my friends' dads seemed so normal, and so did mine. My dad seemed just like everyone else's. None of my friends ever mentioned this sort of thing happening to them, so I never said anything to anybody either."

"You couldn't talk to your mother or your friends." Amy restated. "It doesn't sound like you had anyone to talk to."

"I didn't. I had absolutely no one. For eight years, I've had no one."

"Now you have us," Jill emphasized.

"Yes, as incredible as it sounds, you are the first ones I've had to talk to in all of these years."

"I didn't mean to interrupt your story," Jill assured. "Please continue."

"I became my father's wife. Last night while I was awake all night thinking about this, I realized that somewhere the roles got reversed. Instead of my father looking after his daughter, I became the parent and started looking after my father. But it's even more complicated than that. I wasn't really the parent looking after the child; I was the wife looking after the husband. Do you understand?"

There were nods from the class, and she continued.

"When he went back to work, I took on all of the household chores. He had begun drinking heavily sometime during those years—probably the original decline in his business was due to his drinking. He's had many jobs in the past five years, but he doesn't seem to hold them very long. It must be due to his drinking because he really is a very brilliant man. Everyone always likes him and wants him to succeed. He's a fun person who people like to be around."

"It sounds like you really care about your father, but how has this affected your life, Sonja?" Bill asked.

"I've always been different, or at least, I've felt different from kids my own age. I've never had a best friend I could tell everything to—no one to whisper secrets to. I've never trusted anyone before."

"In what other ways has it affected you?" Jill asked.

"At one point last year, I tried to make myself very ugly, so he wouldn't come near me. I stopped wearing make-up, and I pulled my hair straight back. But I soon found that looking unattractive didn't matter to him.

"My mother and father live in the same house, but there doesn't seem to be any feeling of love between the two of them. When there's a problem, father always takes my side and mom always sides with my brother.There's usually a lot of screaming, and then father goes into the den, turns on the TV and starts drinking."

When Sonja paused, Sarah asked, "What do you think your mother would say if you told her your story now, as you've told us?"

"She wouldn't believe it. I've tried to tell her many times before, but I've never been able to. I think I realize that she wouldn't believe me because she would feel very guilty if she did. Sometimes, I've wondered if she hasn't suspected this because she's gone to the extreme in protecting me other ways. It's almost like she has to prove to herself that she takes care of me. For example, she won't let me stay out at night past 10 p.m., no matter what."

"How do you feel about your mother now?" Mae asked.

"I feel very confused. My father has always made my

mother out to be the bad witch of the house, so I've been horrible to her at times. He's always told me that I didn't have to do what she said, that he'd protect me."

At that moment the bell sounded and there was an immediate surge toward Sonja to give her hugs and words of support.

"You're very brave, Sonja, to tell us your story," Mary said. "If you need to talk after school or tonight, call me."

"If you'd like to get away from your home for a couple of days, you can sleep over at my house. Mom won't mind," assured June.

The words of encouragement and support continued until the students had to rush to their next classes.

"Sonja, why don't we talk further in my office," I said as I gathered up my papers and prepared to leave the room.

"I know you have to report this, Mrs. Sturkie," Sonja said, "and that's all right with me. As I said, I know my father needs help, but I can't report him myself. I still love my father."

"Of course, you do," I reassured.

"I knew when I decided to tell the class I'd be opening myself up to a lot of pain. Now my father will know that I've told, and he'll be furious at me. My mother will know, and she'll deny everything. But in spite of this, I'm still glad that, after all of these years, I don't have to keep this secret any longer. It's O.K. to report it, just as long as you do it—and I don't have to."

"Yes, I'll do it right away," I said as we entered my office, and I reached for the phone.

A female police officer arrived within the next fifteen minutes. I could tell by the sensitive way she talked to Sonja and the attention she placed on every detail that she was knowledgeable and well-prepared to handle incest cases.

After she finished talking to Sonja, the officer asked me to call Mrs. Blake, Sonja's mother, and ask her to come to the school. She arrived shortly.

Sonja was right about her mother—after she learned what had happened, she was furious, and she did deny everything.

"How could you do this to your family?" Mrs. Blake asked as she glared at her daughter.

"Mother, this has been going on for years. It's not something that I did to my family. It is something that is being done to me."

"I don't believe it. I don't believe it for one minute," Mrs. Blake snapped back, her carefully shaped eyebrows burrowing into a frown. "Your father is a very decent, honorable man. He would never do such a perverted thing."

"Mother, I know that it's hard for you to accept this, but whether or not you accept it, the fact remains that it's true."

"That is what I will not accept. For some reason, you want to get back at your father and me, and you're using this sick way to do it. You just want to hurt us."

"That's not true, mother. I love you and I love father, but I can't continue to live the lie I'm living, I want the chance for a normal life like my friends—have boyfriends, go out on dates. I want a different life than what I have now."

"And what about your father? What are you doing to his life?"

"Mother, father needs professional help. He's needed it for a long time. He also needs help with his drinking problem. You know, yourself, he can't hold a job for more than a few months. Maybe he'll be forced to get help now."

"Sonja, I will never believe you. I know you are making

this up."

Sonja shook her head, but seemed to sense that more words would not change her mother's mind.

Turning to the officer, Mrs. Blake asked, "What's going to happen to my husband?"

"There's an officer talking to your husband now. We're going to ask him to move out of your home for the next few weeks. If he will not do this voluntarily, then we will have to take Sonja and her brother into custody and place them in a child protection shelter until this goes to court."

Anger seemed to explode across Mrs. Blake's face as she said, "My husband can move in with his brother."

The following day Sonja came to class looking as if she had not slept for two nights. The redness of her eyes was the only color on her pale face.

She spoke with a weary voice, "This is harder than I ever anticipated."

"Tell us about it," Sue encouraged.

"I knew mother wouldn't believe me, but I guess I was hoping somewhere there would be a glimmer of belief—but there isn't. She and my brother yelled and screamed at me until midnight for telling."

She paused and continued, "Before when they ganged up on me, father has always been there to take my side and stick up for me. Now he's at my uncle's, and there's no one for me. As crazy as this may sound, I guess I miss my father."

"It sounds like you need to get out of the house for a couple of days and get some rest. How about coming to my house?" Judy offered.

"I'd like that, and I think my mother would like it too. Maybe we need a little vacation from each other."

The following week Sonja reported she had spent three

days at Judy's house, and she'd had time to think things out.

"During the first couple of days I really wondered if I'd done the right thing by revealing what was going on," she said. "I really felt guilty that I was causing so much pain for my father and mother and my brother. But when I got away from the house and looked at everything objectively, I knew I had made the only decision I could make."

"Have you heard from your father?" Bill asked.

"I haven't talked to him directly, but mother has. She told us that he is getting psychological counseling twice a week, and he's going to AA meetings three times a week."

"What about your mother? How is she?" Amy asked.

"She still says she doesn't believe me, but I think she really does. She just won't admit it—that way she doesn't have to feel guilty."

"And you? How are you, Sonja?" Kim asked.

"I'm coming along. I saw a therapist for the first time yesterday, and I'll be seeing him on a weekly basis.

"I know that it's going to take a long time for all of us to be normal—whatever that means—and we may never reach it. But at least, we're on the road—headed in the right direction."

As I listened to Sonja speak, I wondered about the other four victims Dr. Rice said would be in this class if the statistics were true. I wondered if they would ever come forth and start on that road to recovery. If they did, I knew there would be a peer counseling class ready to stand by and support them.

CHAPTER NINE

Death— No Immunity to the Trauma

"Have you heard?" Jessica asked as she entered the first period class. Something about her voice alerted me to the fact that she was bringing bad news, but before I could answer, she spoke again, "Heidi died last night."

"I'm so sorry," I began.

But Jessica rushed on, "Everyone I've talked to on campus this morning is upset. It'll be hard for some of the kids who were close to her to get through the day."

The other students were arriving in class, and all the talk before the bell sounded was about Heidi.

As soon as class began, Sue raised her hand and asked, "May we please use today to prepare for the counseling that's ahead of us in the next few days?"

"Yes, I was going to suggest that very thing," I said.

"I need to talk more about how to reach out to Heidi's friends," Ben confessed. "When we covered our unit on

'Death and Dying,' I thought I was ready to help other students learn to accept it, but now that it pertains to somebody we all know, I feel unsure of myself.''

''That's normal under the circumstances,'' I assured. ''I imagine others in the class also have a need to talk about their feelings this morning.''

''I don't understand why it had to be Heidi,'' Pam's voice quivered as she spoke.

All eyes seemed to focus on Pam as they realized that she and Heidi had been friends since elementary school days.

Pam continued, ''Heidi was improving. Just a few days ago she told me she was feeling better than she'd felt since before the doctors discovered she had cancer.''

''I thought she looked better too,'' Sue volunteered. ''Her hair had grown back, and the short, curly style she had looked good. Does anyone know for sure what happened?''

''I talked to her on the phone the night before last, and she told me she was going back into the hospital yesterday for more tests,'' Pam said. ''I didn't think anything was wrong though. She always came back when she went into the hospital. But this time she didn't.''

The echo of Pam's voice seemed to permeate the room and instill a finality to the previous statement.

Heidi would not be back.

As an adult and someone who had dealt with death, it was still difficult for me to realize that I'd never again pass Heidi on campus and be greeted with her wide smile and cheerful hello. While I'd never had her as a student in class or as a counselee, I felt that I knew her. She was a person who was friendly to everyone, and her cheerfulness in the face of adversity endeared her to students and faculty alike.

''Let's talk about our own feelings first,'' I said, ''and

then we will talk about how we'll be available to others when they need to talk."

"I'd like to begin,"Jessica said. "Right now I'm feeling like this can't be true. I know that it's real, but I don't want to believe it."

"That's exactly what I was thinking," Valerie quickly responded."I'm in the denial stage. I remember when we studied about it, I wondered how anyone could deny something when they knew it to be a fact. Now I understand. "

It was Pam's turn to talk, "I feel an emptiness, a gnawing inside. I feel almost sick to my stomach. My best friend will never come to my house again. We will never go shopping together, or go to the movies, or share secrets. I think that I may even be a little angry at her for dying and leaving me. We'd been friends for so long, and I guess I thought we'd be friends for the rest of our lives. Now we can't do all the things we'd plan to do together—like be college roommates. We didn't even get to say goodbye."

Raising both hands to cover her face, she sobbed in a muffled voice, "Why, Heidi? Why did you die and leave me?"

Allison reached over from her chair beside Pam's and gave her a hug. Sometimes when words seem inadequate, a hug is just the support we need and most appreciate.

Continuing around the circle, Hank was the next one to speak, "I feel depressed. Last year my father had a heart attack and died suddenly. One minute he was fine, and the next minute, he was dead. It took me a long time to get over his death—I don't know if I'm over it completely yet. Heidi's dying suddenly, even though she'd been ill for over a year, brings back some of the feelings I had last year—especially the feelings of depression."

Ann spoke from across the circle, "I can relate to that,

Hank. My father died when I was only six, and sometimes I can hardly remember him at all. But I get very depressed when someone who I know dies because I begin thinking of my dad. It makes me sad just thinking of all of the years I've been cheated out of having a father. I'm feeling that same way again."

"I just wish I could do something to have Heidi back with us for at least a few more months," Gary said somberly. "Heidi invited me to the backwards dance last month, and I was planning on inviting her to the prom. We talked about the prom one day last week after civics class, but I didn't ask her to go even though I sensed she'd like for me to."

"You thought you had plenty of time to invite her," Pam said understandingly.

"Yes, that's exactly right. I thought I had all the time in the world. The prom is still two months away."

His voice dropped as he continued, "Now I'd do just about anything if I could just have a little while to make up for those times I've been so thoughtless. I'd work hard, save my money, rent a limo, and take her to the prom in style. I'd do anything if she could be here until the end of the school year."

"I'm sorry, Gary, I don't think I realized you and Heidi were dating," Jessica said.

"We weren't really dating—we just kind of had an understanding that when something came along we needed a date for, we'd go with each other. She felt comfortable with me. I felt comfortable with her."

Gary paused briefly and then continued, "We never talked about her illness—and certainly not about dying. Now that I look back, she might have wanted to do that sometime, and I may not have been sensitive enough to pick up the signals. If only I had a few more months, I'd be a better friend."

Melanie spoke, "I know what you mean, Gary. I wish I'd helped Heidi last week with her calculus. She'd gotten behind because she'd been absent for a couple of days the week before. I was so busy doing a lot of things for myself that I didn't offer to help. However, I think Heidi forgave us all for our shortcomings because she was that kind of a person. I think now we must forgive ourselves and accept Heidi's death. I feel that's what she would want us to do."

The dialogue continued for a while longer and then I spoke, "I hope all of you have been listening very carefully today. By talking out your own feelings with each other, you have helped yourselves. But you've also done something else. The different emotions you've expressed are representative of the kinds of feelings you'll be hearing on campus. Today I've heard you talk about feelings of denial, anger, depression, bargaining, and acceptance. These are the same feelings other students on campus will be experiencing. A student may feel that something is wrong with him or her for having some of these feelings. In other words, someone may feel guilty for feeling angry. Because you recognize that anger is a normal reaction, you'll be able to be a more effective peer counselor.

"Some of those affected by Heidi's death may not be able to express their feelings. Remember most students have not learned to verbalize feelings as you have. You may need to listen to what the student is not saying. Watch for body language and unusual behavior. If you see a student all alone at brunch or lunch, you might offer to sit with him or her and be available.

"Just remember, having someone nearby is very important during times like these. But if any of you are uncomfortable dealing with this subject, keep in mind, you don't have to be available to counsel others.

"Tomorrow there will be a notice in the daily bulletin inviting all students who would like to participate in our discussion about death and dying to get their teacher's permission to join our class—even if they would just like to sit and watch. We'll listen to the visitors tomorrow in the same way that you've listened to each other today.

"I would also suggest that a large number of you wear your peer counseling shirts for the next few days. You need to be very visible on campus for anyone who's looking for a peer counselor.

"I know I need not remind you to be available for each other. I will be in my office until late after school if any of you would like to talk."

The following day, our class was packed with visitors. What a contrast to the meeting that was held a few years previously when another student died. There was no peer counseling on campus then, and a therapist in the community was invited to conduct discussion sessions at noontime for anyone interested in talking about death and loss. She had come for three days consecutively, but the response was very small. When I looked around the room and saw all of the visitors this day, my belief was reaffirmed that students identify with each other and will participate to a greater extent when the faces leading the discussions are familiar ones.

We made the circle wider to accommodate our visitors, but there were not sufficient chairs for everyone. When the seats were all filled, peer counselors and guests alike sat on the floor in the middle of the circle.

Because this was the first time many of the guests had visited our class, we made sure they knew they didn't have to speak. The peer counselors started the class off by discussing some of the things they'd learned earlier in the semester about death and dying. Then they began to talk about their own feelings. It wasn't long before the visitors started raising their hands and joining in the discussion.

Kristy was one of the first visitors to speak, "This is the only time in my life I've been able to sit down and talk about someone dying. When my grandmother died last year, I was treated like a little child who had to be protected. When I entered the living room and overheard Mom and Dad talking about the funeral arrangements, they quickly changed the subject once they realized that I was there. I asked my aunt about the color of the dress grandmother was to be buried in, and she told me that everything was taken care of and not to worry about anything. In other words, I wasn't even supposed to think about death, much less talk about it."

"How do you feel talking about it now?" Jessica asked.

"It's a relief to be able to express my feelings and not have to hide them. I wanted to tell my mother how much I really missed my grandmother, and I'd like to talk to her about some of the good memories of things my grandmother and I did together. It would've helped to talk about it. Just as it helps now to talk about Heidi's death."

Tom joined in, "I never thought Heidi would die. She went into the hospital at other times and missed a couple of weeks of school, but she always came back. I live just down the street from her, and I knew she went into the hospital this time—but I thought she'd come back. When I passed her house yesterday, I had this feeling I wanted to go in and say something to her parents, but I didn't know what to say.''

''What would you like to say to them?'' Valerie asked.

''I'd like to say that I'm sorry Heidi died and that I thought she was really a neat person.''

''I think they'd like to hear those exact words,'' Valerie assured. ''I think they would like to know how important Heidi was to all of us.''

''Would you go to their house with me?'' Tom asked.

''I'd be glad to,'' Valerie said. ''I'd been thinking of going myself.''

''What about Heidi's little sister, Kay?'' Adam, another guest asked. ''I've wondered about her. Has anyone talked to her to see how she's doing?''

''I have,'' Pam responded. ''Heidi and I were very good friends and we spent a lot of time at each other's houses. I talked to Kay a lot when I was visiting Heidi. Yesterday I went over, and Kay and I just sat on the front porch. Neither one of us said much, but we were there for each other. It felt good.''

Mike spoke next, ''When my brother was killed on a motorcycle last year, we had a lot of people around for the first week, and then there was no one. I think it's important to visit the family even two or three weeks after the funeral because that's when all the relatives have gone back home and the loneliness really sets in. I needed someone to talk to then—even more than the first week.''

''That's a very good point,'' I said. ''Kay needs to be remembered not only now, but also in the weeks to come.''

''I've never been to a funeral,'' Wanda, another guest, confessed. ''I really want to go to Heidi's funeral tomorrow, but I guess I'm afraid. Could we talk about what happens at a funeral?''

Steve responded, "I've been to several funerals, and they've all been different. Each church has its own type of service and sometimes even the same religious faiths vary the service to accommodate the family's wishes. Heidi was Methodist, and last year I attended a funeral at the Methodist church. Basically, a few songs were sung, the minister spoke, and then everyone walked by the open casket to pay their last respects."

"I've never been to a funeral that had an open casket," Evan said.

"It's up to the family whether it's open or closed," Amy volunteered.

This forthright and honest conversation continued until the bell sounded. Some visitors had joined in and talked openly and freely. Others had sat quietly and only listened. No one had been pressured to say anything.

After class, one of the girls who hadn't said a word, approached me, introduced herself, and said, "Thank you, Mrs. Sturkie, for inviting us today. I feel so much better after hearing that others are feeling the same way I do. I see now how important peer counseling is. I hope that I can take it next year."

"Thank you for coming," I said. "I'm glad being here today helped. We'd love to have you in peer counseling next year."

The peer counselors were very busy for the next few days. Going to the funeral proved to be a very emotional experience for many students on campus, and the peer counselors were sought out heavily before and after the service. We had another day when visitors were invited to join our circle to discuss their feelings concerning death—and again the room was full.

Two weeks later, we were in the middle of another unit completely unrelated to death, when word came to us that one of the large hardware stores in town had burned and four people had been killed. It was a freak accident. A fire started on the roof, reached the paint department and trapped four people in a blazing inferno. One of the victims was a boy who had graduated from our high school only two years previously. He was working part-time, while attending the nearby community college. Again, a student who was well-known in the community had died, and the effect of his death was felt by many on campus.

"I just don't understand," Pam said. "I haven't gotten over Heidi's death and now Neil gets killed."

"Did you know Neil well?" Sue asked.

"He was my brother's best friend, and he was at our house a lot. His home life was crummy, but he was working so hard to make a good life for himself—and he was doing it."

"I heard he'd already been accepted at UCLA," Steve said.

"That's right, he had," Pam confirmed. "He had totally supported himself for the past two years, and he earned a 3.3 grade point average at the same time. I was so proud of him. It just isn't fair. It seems like all the good people die."

"It sounds as if you are really hurting," Bill stated. "Is there anything we can do to help?"

"You are helping by just being here for me—and understanding. I don't think I could go through the school day if I didn't have all of you to understand."

For the next few weeks, the peer counselors found themselves again spending hours of time listening to peers who were experiencing grief, some for the first time. The counseling did not take place only at school. Sometimes the students made it through the busy school day fine; but after school, when the house was empty and they were alone, they would pull out the list of peer counselors' phone numbers and contact a person who would listen and understand their feelings.

By being able to use the word "death" and talk honestly and unashamedly about their feelings, the students were able to work through their grief and fears.

Teenagers experience the same feelings of coming to grips with their own immortality that adults do when someone dies. Too often adults believe teenagers are too young to worry about these things. They don't connect fear of dying with young people. However, teenagers are not immune to these fears.

Pam voiced her concerns during an "I feel" session. She began, "Up until a month ago, I never thought about death at all. No one I knew had ever died. Then two of my very good friends died within weeks of each other. Suddenly all I could think about was dying. If my two friends who were seventeen and nineteen could die, then so could I. At that point I began to wonder if I, too, would die young. Why should they die instead of me? Maybe I should look at my life differently. Maybe I should realize that when people say, 'Life is fragile and there are no guarantees,' they're right."

"Has talking about it in this class been helpful to you?" Peter asked.

"It's kept me sane," Pam replied. "Being able to talk out my feelings has given me an understanding of death that I didn't have before. I think I can accept it now as a part of life. It makes life even more special now that I realize how quickly relationships can come to an end."

''I agree, Pam,'' Kevin said. ''I feel the same way. By helping other kids deal with their feelings, I've come to a better understanding of life and death myself.''

Pam concluded, ''I wish every student on campus had the opportunity to talk with someone about death and dying. It's something that will touch each of our lives—whether it be a friend or a relative. It's so much easier to deal with, if we aren't afraid to talk about it.''

CHAPTER TEN

Parents and Kids— If Only They Would Listen

"You gotta be kidding," Karen said with a wide grin and a look that seemed to say, "Let 's deal with reality."

"I'm not kidding," I said. "You want to go to the prom with Eddie and you need your mother's permission. Therefore, talking to your mother is necessary in getting to do what you want to do."

"But I can't talk to my mother," this beautiful girl with red hair and green eyes said. "She doesn't know how to listen."

"I can identify with that," Mark chimed in. "I don't think my mom or dad know the definition of the word."

Sue contributed, "My parents try to listen, and I'm sure they think they do a good job— but honestly sometimes I think they don't hear a word I say."

"I wish you'd teach a peer counseling class for parents, Mrs. Sturkie," Cammie suggested. "If my mom and dad could learn all the skills we learn in this class, then we could communicate—I mean really communicate."

I responded, "I talk to parents in my counseling office, and I know they want that too. They want to really communicate with their kids. I've thought about teaching a peer counseling class for parents. I like the idea, and maybe sometime I'll do that. But until that comes about, it's going to be up to you to work on communication with your parents. I want you to make a real effort to put your skills into practice in your own home."

"Are you asking us to teach our parents how to communicate?" Kara inquired.

"The best teaching is often done by example," I responded. "I'm asking you to be an example of what you've learned. Be a good listener, don't interrupt, don't judge, don't offer advice. See if you can communicate with your parents by doing these things, then perhaps they'll follow your example. Try it tonight and we'll talk about it tomorrow."

As the bell sounded and the students left class with their assignments, I breathed a silent prayer that the parents would be responsive to these students who were testing their wings in the most difficult territory of all—their own homes.

The following day many were eager to share their experiences. When I asked who would like to talk first, at least ten hands shot up all at the same time.

Betsy seemed to be waving her hand with such energy and enthusiasm I decided to call on her first.

She responded with, "You will never believe my conversation with my mom last night—we actually talked for over an hour. I still don't believe it myself because the most we ever say to each other usually doesn't last more than ten minutes. But last night I was determined."

"Tell us about it," Jane encouraged.

"Well, I did a little preparation for it in advance. You know my mom and I live alone, and she works. Yesterday afternoon I went home after school and cooked dinner for us. I mean, I really cooked—not just a hamburger or hot dogs like I usually make when mom asks me to cook. I made lasagna from scratch. It took me a couple of hours, but it was worth it."

"Sounds good," Jimmy said. "Why didn't you invite me over?"

Betsy made a face at Jimmy and continued, "And I served hot French bread and a green salad with it."

"No wonder your mother listened; she must have been in shock," Jimmy continued.

"No, she listened because I asked her to," Betsy responded.

"When she came in the door, I had the table all set. As soon as she sat down, I approached her in a straightforward way. I said, 'Mom, I want us to talk while we 're eating—really talk.'

"Mom's face went kind of pale," Betsy said with a giggle. "I think she thought I was going to tell her something dreadful—that I'd failed a class or was pregnant.

"'Talk about what?' She shot back.

"'Let's talk about communicating with each other,' I said. And from that point on we talked and we listened to each other. I told her about the things I'd learned in this class, and she was really impressed.

"When we finished our meal and our talk, mom gave me a hug and thanked me for making her evening so nice. She suggested that we have talks at least once a week. Mom even offered to cook for our next special evening."

"Your mom sounds real cool," Connie responded.

" I'd never thought about it until last night, but, yes, I think you're right. She really is a cool mom. I've found out how much I enjoy spending time with her. It's great when we can have the opportunity to talk and actually listen to each other."

"I wish what I have to report could be as positive," Karen remarked almost to herself.

"Let's hear your report next, Karen," I said.

"I really needed to talk to my mom about going to the prom with Eddie, so I asked her if we could talk while she was cooking dinner. Our conversation went something like this:

"I began, 'Mom, there's this nice boy at school I know, and he's asked me to go to the prom.'

"'Do I know him?' she asked without looking up from peeling the potatoes.

"'No, I've never gone out with him before,' I answered.

"'You said he's a nice boy?'

"'Yes, he is. He's well-liked on campus by both kids and teachers. In fact, he's a class officer; and, also, he's one of our best basketball players.'

"'I guess it's O.K. with me, but you've got to earn your own money to buy your prom dress.'

"'I know, mom. That won't be a problem. I already have most of it saved.'

"Gathering the lettuce, tomatoes, green onions and carrots from the refrigerator, mom started to make the salad. The conversation was over as far as she was concerned. I was tempted to let it drop too—but I knew when she found out that I hadn't told her everything about Eddie, she'd probably ground me.

''Mustering up all the courage I could find, I blurted out in one breath, 'Eddie is not Caucasian.'

''I saw the tomato mom was slicing drop from her hands and bounce on the lettuce in the salad bowl. Her eyes shot up at me, and I felt like a dagger was piercing me. I hate it when mom looks at me like that. I feel condemned to a nothing status.

''She said four words, 'No, you can't go.'

''I responded, 'But, mom, you'd like him if you got to know him. I know you would.'

'''I don't want to hear another word about it. The subject is closed.' As if to emphasize what she was saying, she took the salad dressing from the refrigerator and slammed the door shut with so much force that the china in the cabinets next to it rattled.

''I knew no matter what I tried to say, I would not be able to get through to her. She had made up her mind and that was that.''

''It sounds like the two of you have a different opinion about dating outside your own race,'' Sam remarked.

''That is true; we do. And I respect her opinion. But I would like to be able to sit and discuss why she feels the way she does and why I feel like I do.''

''Has she ever discussed her feelings or allowed you to tell her about yours?'' Steve asked.

''No, not really. It's something that she presumes needs no discussion.''

''Is this the way she handles other decisions too?'' Greg asked.

''Usually. It's like she's safe if she closes the door, and doesn't allow the conversation to continue. She doesn't have to listen to any opinions other than her own.

"Some day, I feel I'll rebel against doing what she wants—and I'm not the rebellious type. I just can't stand having ultimatums given without any explanation."

"Karen, have you tried talking to her about controversial issues at a different time?" I asked.

"What do you mean?"

"Would it be easier if you brought up the subject of dating on a day when you weren't asking to go some place with a boy? Maybe at a time when your mother is relaxed and doesn't feel she has to make an immediate decision."

"I don't know if it would make any difference with my mom. She would probably still say 'no.'"

"I'm not talking about whether she says yes or no. I'm looking for a way that you and your mother can talk openly and honestly. From what I've heard you say, I think you want that more than anything else."

"I do. I want us to talk about our feelings and be able to explain why we feel the way we do. I'm nearly 17, and I'd like to be treated like an adult instead of a child."

"That will be the day," Ellis remarked.

"What do you mean?" Karen asked.

"Oh, I wasn't referring to you, Karen. I meant that will be the day, if my old man ever treats me like an adult."

"Are you and your father having more difficulties?" I asked.

Ellis had shared with the class a few days previously that his father kicked him out of the house for coming home past his curfew. After spending the night at a friend's house, he'd gone back home the next day after school and found all the locks on his house had been changed. Again he had to spend the night at his friend's house.

"'More difficulties' doesn't even half-way describe what we're having. 'War' would be a better word for our situation."

"You weren't able to talk to your father last night?" I asked.

"I tried. I really tried. I called him at his office two times. Both times he was in a meeting, so I was told. I left word for him to call me, but he never did. Then last night after dinner I called him at home. He answered the phone, but when he found out it was me he said, 'I don't have anything to say to you, kid.' And he hung up.

"I've got to get some clean clothes from that house. I've worn these jeans now for three days."

"Ellis, I think this is more than a break down in communication. I think you'd better come to my office after class and let me call your father."

Ellis nodded his approval.

Connie raised her hand, and I acknowledged her.

"I tried to talk to both of my parents yesterday," she began, "but as usual it seemed to be the wrong time."

"What happened?" Steve asked.

"It's the same story all the time. My parents are great parents—really super people—but they don't have time to talk to me. They are pillars of the community and are in constant demand to be at parties and fund raising events."

"Sounds like they're very popular," Sonja injected.

"They are. People enjoy being around them—but so do I."

"Could you tell them that?" Tom asked.

"I try. I tried again last night, but it didn't work. Mom got home from work first and I said, 'Mom, do you have a few minutes to talk?'

"'Gee, I'd like to,' she responded, 'but I've got to take my shower and get dressed before your father gets home. We are due at the chamber banquet at 7:00 o'clock.'

"'That's what I wanted to talk to you about,' I said as I followed Mom to her bedroom.

"'About the chamber banquet?' She called out over her shoulder as she disappeared into the dressing room.

"'No, about us not having time to talk any more.'

"'I know, Sweetie, but there isn't time tonight to talk about not having time to talk. I know you understand though. This banquet is very important—your father and I are sitting at the head table—and we can't arrive late. We'll talk some time soon. I promise.'

"I heard the shower water start to run, and I leaned backward on mom's bed. I needed time to think. What should I be doing differently? Apparently I wasn't handling this correctly.

"Almost as if she knew I hadn't left her room, she stuck her head out of the bathroom door and said as she quickly pushed her hair under her shower cap, 'Remember what you wanted to tell me. We'll talk tomorrow.'"

Bill asked, "Will you be able to talk to your mom today?"

"Probably not. I checked the calendar on the refrigerator this morning, and it had 'dinner at the Simpsons' marked on today's date."

After a brief moment of thought, Connie went on to explain, "I really don't resent my parents having an active social life, but it gets pretty lonely around the house, especially since my sister left this past year for college."

"Your problem sounds somewhat similar to mine," Vicki volunteered. "My parents aren't as social as yours, but they're away on trips together much of the time."

''Do you have anyone else in your household?'' Connie asked.

''No, that's the thing,'' Vicki answered. ''I have four older brothers and sisters, and before they went away to college, mom was home all of the time. Dad traveled frequently then, and I can remember mom saying that one day she would get to go with him. But I thought she'd wait until all of us had left home.

''Since I'm the last child at home, I guess mom thinks I can take care of myself. Which, basically, I think I can. But it would be a whole lot easier for me if she'd continue to parent me until I got out of high school.''

''You two don't know how easy you have it,'' Wayne spoke out in a forceful voice.

''What do you mean?'' Connie asked.

''You two are left alone in a nice home. You are free to make your own decisions, do what you want, not worry about what's going to happen next.''

''Maybe you'd better explain. I'm afraid I'm not following you very well,'' Connie informed him.

''What I mean is, I'd change places with either of you anytime. You may be lonely, but you don't have to worry about a drunken father coming in at any moment and wanting to start a fight.''

''Your father drinks heavily?'' Vicki asked.

''My dad is an alcoholic, and ever since mom died he stops by the bars after work. I never know if he is coming home at 7 p.m. or at midnight. The thing I do know is that whenever he comes home, he'll be drunk.''

''That must be hard on you,'' Vicki sympathized.

''It's like living in a battle zone. I think he must subconsciously be angry that I'm at home and mom's not. He must know that I miss her as much as he does. If only he'd come home sober once, just once, so we could sit down and talk."

Pausing before he continued, he said softly, "I wasn't able to do my communication assignment last night. Dad came in about 9 p.m. Drunk. I knew not to try to talk to him when he was like that. He would just become more abusive."

Janet raised her hand. When acknowledged she said, "I guess we all have problems in one way or another. My mother is constantly comparing me to my older sisters.

"Last night I tried to talk to mom and ask her about going to the movies with Ben this week-end. We got off to a good start because I opened the conversation with something positive. I told her about making an 'A' in French. She was very pleased. We actually talked for ten or fifteen minutes, and then I brought up the subject of Ben.

"'I won't have you turn out like your two older sisters,' she said abruptly. She was referring to the fact that both of my sisters got pregnant in high school and had abortions. One sister had two, in fact.

"'You're smarter than either one of them are,' Mom continued. 'You have a bright future ahead. I'm not going to allow you to date boys until you're out of high school.'

"'What?' I asked in disbelief. She was talking about no dates for the next two years. I had always thought she would let me date when I turned sixteen.

"'You heard me right,' she said. 'If I don't let you date, then I won't have to worry about you. All I want for you is a good life—and not one like your sisters have.'

"I tried to explain to her that I'm not like my sisters. I want more for myself too. But I never got a chance to talk about it. She is convinced that my destiny is doomed if I go out with a boy. It would be so nice if my sisters hadn't messed things up. Now I have to live with their mistakes. If only my mother would listen to me when I tell her that I'm me—not them."

"What will you do about dating?" Bill asked. "Surely you expect to go to the prom before you graduate."

"Of course, I do. I'll keep trying to communicate my feelings to my mother. I hope she'll see she doesn't need to worry about me. I only wish she would hear what I'm saying now—it would be so much easier."

"My problem is not nearly as great as yours, Janet," Zak spoke up. "But what you said about wishing she would listen is the same thing I feel—about both of my parents."

"In what way do they not listen?" Janet asked .

"They just want to lecture and give advice. My parents are really great people, and they do have a lot of wisdom that I don't have. But, sometimes, I just want to talk and come to my own solutions."

"Could you give us an example?" Leslie asked.

"I can tell you what happened last night.

"I wanted to talk to them about not going out for the basketball team this year. They were both in the den relaxing, so I thought the time was right.

"Dad was sitting in the recliner, reading the newspaper; and mom was watching TV and doing needlepoint. I opened the conversation with, 'Hey, Dad, Mom, do you have a few minutes for some stimulating conversation with your son?'

"Dad responded as he put the paper down, 'Of course, we always enjoy talking with you.'

"Mom reached for the remote control and clicked off the T.V. 'What is the topic of this stimulating conversation?' She asked.

"'I was just thinking about my busy schedule this year,

and I thought I'd like to explore some possibilities to lighten the load.'

"'You'll need all of those classes you're taking to get into a good college,' Dad said. 'I don't see how you can even consider dropping any classes.'

"Oh no, I wasn't thinking of dropping a class," I said. "I'd like to explore other possibilities for giving me more time to keep up the grades in those classes."

"'You could give up your Saturday job working in the vet's office,' Mother suggested. She has never liked the idea of my wanting to be a veterinarian. A medical doctor or a lawyer sounds more prestigious to her.

"'Oh, I wouldn't want to do that,' I said. 'I feel that experience will be a plus when I apply to vet school after college.'

"'Well, the only other possibility would be to give up sports,' Dad said jokingly.

"Before I could say, 'Let's talk about that,' he quickly went on.

"'Of course, that's out of the question. You'll be a starter on the basketball team this year, and you'll probably score as many points as Dick Jones' boy.'

"'Dad, I'll never be half-way as good as Keith Jones. He's a natural athlete, and I'm not. He'll probably get a scholarship to play in college.'

"Dad was determined. 'For years Dick Jones and I have been playing golf together and talking about our sons. You may not be quite as good as Keith is, but I know you're going to look good out there this year.'

"'Dad, I think playing is fun, but that's all it is to me, just fun. I'm not dedicated to the game like Keith is. He eats, drinks, and breathes to play basketball—it's the most important thing in his life. And it's not the most important thing in my life.'

"'Your father and I don't expect you to dedicate your life to any sport,' Mom said. 'All we want is for you to do your best. We won't ask anymore than that.'

"I felt rather brave at this point and decided to spring it on them, 'Well, I'm actually thinking about not going out for the team this year.'

"With that statement, Dad's reclining chair shot to the upright, feet-on-the-floor position.

"'I don't believe what I just heard,' he shouted. 'What's wrong with you, boy? Are you turning out to be some kind of a sissy? Are the workouts too tough? Are you getting lazy?'

"He shot the questions at me so fast, all I could do was shake my head.

"'It's not any of those things, Dad,' I tried to tell him. 'I just want more time to work on biology, calculus, British literature, German, and civics. I would really like a 3.5 grade point average this semester.'

"'You know your mother and I are all for that too, but you have to learn to work under pressure and prioritize your time. Why, when I was your age and in high school I had to work at a part-time job twenty hours a week to help my mother out. At the same time I was taking a full load AND playing on the basketball team that went to the state championships. Did I ever tell you about the time we were tied with Seagoville with only five seconds to play, and I stole the ball?'

"I'd heard that story no less than 100 times, and I nodded my head—but it didn't stop him from going through the whole thing all over again.

"That game reminded him of two other games, and he went into great detail about how he had played with a sprained ankle one time and the flu the other time, but he persevered and his team won."

"What did you do?" Steve asked.

"I sat there like I was listening, but I had actually tuned him out. I was thinking about my civics assignment."

"Did you ever get to talk about your feelings again?" Janet asked.

"No, he wasn't interested in how I felt about it. He was only interested in how he felt about it."

"What about your mother?" Amy asked.

"She would never interrupt my dad or go against what he wanted. They started going together in high school when he was the basketball star, and she was the cheerleader. They got married right out of high school, and she worked to put him through college. She is still the cheerleader, leading the cheers for him."

"What are you going to do about basketball?" Steve asked.

"I don't know yet. I don't want to disappoint Mom and Dad, but I know that I'm an over-achiever, not a brain. I have to spend a lot of time studying if I'm going to be a veterinarian, and that's what I really want to be. I wish Mom and Dad would hear me out when I try to talk to them. They mean well, but they don't listen. I don't think they know how important it is to me to be a vet. If they would only listen, I could share some of my dreams."

"If they would only listen." How often I had heard that same phrase from parents when they were talking about their teenagers.

How ironic that parents and teenagers want the same

thing—to communicate with each other—but so often this is not acccomplished. There must be a solution to the problem.

There is.

Listen.

You may find it.

CHAPTER ELEVEN

Divorce–A Painful Word

"It became my responsibility to get the Christmas tree, and that was the most painful experience of the season," the soft spoken words came slowly and deliberately from the tall, good-looking, sophomore boy sitting in the circle. "It was something I had never had to do–Dad had always done that. The thought of having to do it had never even entered my mind before. Divorce was not supposed to happen in our family."

Divorce. The word uttered more frequently than any other in the "I feel" session. At least half of the class felt the sting of that word on a very personal basis. The other half felt it in their role as friends who listened, cared, consoled.

"Would you like to talk about the tree?" Jenny gently probed. She was aware after being in peer counseling for two years that talking about family problems during the month of December was not easy, but often very helpful.

When the students were able to vent their fears and frustration before the holiday season began, they were better prepared to cope when the more painful days arrived.

''I was so disappointed in that tree,'' Dave continued. ''It wasn't as tall as our previous trees—maybe I'd grown several inches—but I still had a hard time getting it through the door when I got home. Then I couldn't get it in the stand. It may have been like this every year, but I didn't have to deal with it. Dad had always taken care of everything.''

''That was last Christmas, after your dad had just left?'' Scott inquired.

''He'd been gone nearly a year, but that was the first Christmas without him.''

''Were you as surprised when your mom and dad split up, as I was when it happened to mine?'' Sherri asked.

''It was the shock of my life,'' the pain of recalling that time was on Dave's face as he spoke.

''The last two years have really been hard. I can sympathize with anyone who has been through this—,'' his voice dropped; he paused and then continued softly, ''because there is so much pain. I kept asking myself, 'How could something like this happen?' Thirteen years of my life—and then suddenly it's dissipated. It seems to be gone. But now after it's been a little while, I realize it's not over.''

''What did you feel was gone?'' Jill asked with concern in her voice.

''It seemed at the time that it was the end of all of my happiness. All of a sudden, I had to deal with the real world. What a rude awakening. I felt cheated out of getting to finish my childhood.''

Matt, who had been sitting in reflective silence, spoke up, ''I can certainly relate to that. When my dad left, I automatically became the father figure in our home. Anything that needed to be done became my job.''

Dave nodded and then continued, ''I wanted to support my mother too. I felt that we needed each other during those first few months.''

''It sounds like your mother was shocked, too, when your dad left. Did it happen suddenly?'' Sue asked.

''Kind of. I remember one night when dad and mother came home, she was crying. Dad went to the bedroom, and I asked her what was the matter. She was really upset when she said, 'Your father wants to leave us.'

''That was like my worst nightmare coming true. I said, 'I don't think he meant it.' I just couldn't make myself believe it. But the next day, he confirmed that he was leaving.

''Then he didn't leave. I began to think his statement had just been a threat, and I tried to forget it. I think I actually did for a while. Then one day about six months later he moved out.''

Silence penetrated the room. Looking at some of the students, I could see similar memories relived on their faces.

Shirley broke the silence, ''How did you feel the day he left, Dave?''

''Angry. I was very angry. And I think what made me even angrier was when he asked me to help him move his things out of the house. It was beyond ALL comprehension that he would ask me to do a thing like that, so I just left the house for the day.

''When I came back that night and he was gone, it was almost as if he'd died. In fact, during the following months, I went through the same emotions we covered in our unit on 'Death and Dying.' I felt denial at first; I really didn't want to believe it had happened. Then I felt angry; what right did he have to mess up my life? After that came depression, bargaining, and then finally acceptance.''

Eva interrupted, ''My mother moved out five years ago, and I haven't accepted it to this day.'' Her voice conveyed the anger she still felt.

''It hasn't come easy for me either,'' Dave continued. ''I have really worked on it. But there are times I must admit, my acceptance disappears. Like right now when I think about my dad being so far away.

''He left for six months because he had the opportunity to work in a country he'd always wanted to visit. That's fine for him, and I'm glad that he has the opportunity to see new things—but now he isn't here to see me participate in any of the extra-curricular activities at school. I've had a good year, and I've been involved in things I would've liked to have had his support in, especially the school play. I had a major part, and he wasn't able to come to any of the performances.''

''Did you see your dad often before he went on his trip?'' asked Cliff.

''When he first moved into his apartment, I didn't see him very much because I felt guilty—as if I were betraying my mother. Because mother was with me at home and dad was the one who had left, I felt like it was all his fault. Now I realize that probably wasn't right.''

''After a few months you started to see your dad more regularly?'' Scott inquired.

''Yes, but when his girlfriend moved in, I didn't want to go there with her around. That was very painful. In my eyes, he turned from being the father figure into a teenage-like-person. I really didn't know how to handle that, so I stayed away. He and his girl friend have broken up now though. That happened just before he left the country."

"What do you think you've learned from the divorce in your family?" Susan asked.

"I've learned that my life must go on as normally as possible. The first year after the divorce, I stayed home. I made good grades because all I ever did was study. Then the second year I became involved in extracurricular activities, and I began to have a good time.

"I've learned that there really isn't much I can do about the situation between my dad and mom and that I can't assume the guilt for what's happened."

Connie had been listening intensely, and suddenly she blurted out, "I wish I could've sat in a peer counseling class and heard someone say those things when my parents got a divorce. I didn't have anyone to relate to and it was rough on me. I felt a tremendous amount of guilt for what happened in our family."

Dave encouraged, "Would you like to tell us about it?"

"Yes, I'd like to share some of my feelings."

"Go right ahead," Emily said.

"I was 12 years old when it happened, and I knew all the circumstances of my parents' divorce. I was a real curious child, actually to the point of being nosy, and I found a letter from my mom to a man who she was in love with."

"Did you read the letter?" John asked.

"Yes, I read it, and I was really upset because it was written to the father of two of my best friends. My friends were twin sisters, and it was their father my mother was in love with. I knew this secret, but I never told the twins.

"There was a real bond between my father and me, and one day several months later, after I had observed my mother sleeping on the couch at night, I told him about the letter.

I also told him that I had seen my mother go across the street to this man's house. Needless to say, my dad was very upset by this. Apparently he'd known sometime earlier about this other man in my mother's life, but she had promised my father she would never see the man again. When he heard that she'd broken her promise he became very angry.

"He and mother went out for a drive that night, and when they returned dad told me they were getting a divorce.

"I felt responsible. If I hadn't told my dad about seeing her with this man, they wouldn't be getting divorced. At least, that's how I felt in the beginning, and the guilt was awful. I didn't have a peer counseling class to confide in. If I could have talked it out, I would have realized sooner that the marriage was doomed no matter what."

"Doomed? I don't understand," Cindy voiced.

"They were two very different people, and love just wasn't enough to overcome all the problems."

"Did your mother leave right away?" John asked.

"No, it was agreed she would leave in two weeks. However, after the first week, my father felt it was too hard on everyone, so he packed her up and moved her out. It was difficult for him because he still loved her and was very hurt by what had happened.

"But I felt sorry for my mother too, and so guilty over what I'd done that when she moved out, I went with her to spend the night.

"I had a lot of guilt those first few months. I felt guilty if I didn't treat my mother right, and then I felt guilty toward my dad if I spent too much time with my mother. I think they played me against each other a lot during those first few months—and I think they still do to some extent.

"Something else happened to add to all of this. My family belonged to a very close-knit church, and it was a little bit gossipy at times. There were a lot of rumors going around about why my parents split up, and unfortunately, I heard what was being said. I overheard one rumor that hurt very badly. Someone said that my mother was too mentally unstable to handle us kids, that we were terrible children and that we drove her away. This really hit home, and it hurt more than anything anyone could have said. Plus, a neighbor across the street was the sister of the wife of the man mom was in love with, and she started malicious rumors about my mom. So I had all of these ugly lies to deal with both at church and in my neighborhood.

''I think the rumors hurt more than the divorce. People were so vicious. I couldn't understand how they could be so cruel. They treated me like I had the plague. In my church community, people are not supposed to get divorced; therefore, I was not like the rest of the children.

''School was different though. It didn't seem to matter to anyone. A lot of my friends' parents were divorced, and it wasn't a big deal to them that my parents were splitting. At the school I attended then, there was no peer counseling, no one to care, and that can be as cruel as the rumors.''

''That must have been a terrible time in your life,'' Angie said with deep concern.

''It was. I wouldn't want to go through it again. But I survived. I think I was fortunate because I'm naturally a strong person. My younger brother and sister were not, and their lives have turned out very different from mine. When my sister reached junior high, she turned to drugs and sex. My brother has threatened suicide and is still seeing a psychiatrist. Yet, I was the one who had experienced that tremendous amount of guilt.''

Pausing before she continued, she said softly, ''I guess divorce affects us all differently, and its hard to predict which ones it will affect the most.''

''Even though you are stronger than your brother and sister, do you feel it has left any lasting marks on you?'' John asked.

''It's hard for me to talk about it, even after all of this time. Yes, I do still have a lot of scars. I still have unresolved problems, but not the type that keep me from successfully functioning on a day-to-day basis. Mainly, I don't really trust people very much. The reason I don't is because of how people treated me during that time. Now I generally have an optimistic view, but once someone hurts me, I withdraw from that person. I don't like being hurt or rejected. I think I feel so strongly about it because of the divorce—I went through a lot of hurt.''

''If you could talk to a group of parents who were thinking about getting a divorce, what would you tell them?'' Julie asked.

''I'd tell them that it's the children who suffer the most from a divorce. Parents seem to be able to pick up and go on with their lives, but children continue to hurt.''

Silence fell in the room for the next few moments. Then Julie, a petite girl with long, brown hair, spoke.

''I guess divorce does affect each of us differently,'' she said.

''What are you referring to?'' Steve asked.

''I was just thinking as I listened to Dave and Connie that I was affected in a very different way than either of you.

''My mother and father were divorced when I was only a few months old, so I don't remember anything about the divorce itself. I guess you might say I was lucky because I didn't have to go through the crisis of that period. However, my life has certainly been affected by what happened way back then."

"You have a step-father, don't you?" Frances asked.

"Yes, but I didn't for the first six years of my life. That's what made the adjustment so difficult."

"Having a stranger move in created problems?" Jesse phrased his question in such a way that I felt he was making a statement from his own experience.

"It wasn't so much that Mike was a stranger because he had taken me lots of places when he came over to see mom. The three of us had gone to get ice cream cones, to the movies, to the zoo. I really liked Mike at that time."

"Sounds like things changed after the wedding," Steve said.

"They did. It was probably my fault as much as anyone's, but it was very traumatic to me."

"In what way?" Amy asked.

"For seven years I had been the number one priority in my mother's life. She was, and is, a wonderful mother, and she wanted to make sure I got lots of time and attention. Looking back, I realize she may have gone to the extreme in this. But because I didn't have a dad, she tried very hard to make sure I was a happy child. And I was.

"Mom worked to support us, but I knew that when she got home the entire evening would be spent with the two of us doing things together. Mom never made me go to bed before she did because she wanted to make sure we spent plenty of time together."

"I can imagine Mike didn't take too well to that arrangement," John said.

"You're right. As soon as they got married, Mike insisted

that I go to bed by eight o'clock. I think he really thought that I needed the sleep and that mom was being negligent in her duties by letting me stay up so late. But I didn't see it that way. I just thought I was being rejected.

''All of those fun evenings with mom were gone. I can remember crying myself to sleep night after night, week after week. And it was during that time, I made up my mind to get rid of Mike. I thought if he left, things would be like they used to be.

''I had never been a rebellious child, but I became one. The more havoc I created, the more restrictions were put on me— and the more I felt rejected, the more rebellious I became. It was a vicious circle. Finally mom told me that Mike was leaving because all of us were miserable.

''I can remember being so happy when I heard that. Now my life would be like it used to be. But it wasn't. Mom cried a lot, and we didn't have fun any more.

''When Mike moved back in the following month, I didn't mind as much as I had before—but I still resented his taking away the time I thought I should have with my mother.

''That was seven years ago, and I guess I still give Mike a hard time. Just talking about it today has helped me to see things in a little different light. Maybe I have trouble with Mike now because I'm still trying to punish him for marrying mom.''

''Have you and Mike ever sat down and talked about why you don't get along?'' Sue asked.

''No, not really. We have talked about problems, but not about how we feel about each other.''

''Do you think that might be helpful?'' Sue continued to probe.

''Maybe. Mike has his faults, but to be honest, I may still

be acting like a spoiled child. If we could start over on a more mature basis, we might get along better."

"If there is any way to work things out, I'd say you are a lot more fortunate than I am," Barry said.

All eyes turned to the boy with the spiked hair, feathered earring, and leather jacket.

"I didn't think your mom was married," Dale said.

"She isn't," Barry replied. "Hasn't been since she and my old man got divorced four years ago."

"Then I don't understand how I am more fortunate than you are," Julie said.

"Because you don't have to worry about who your mother is out with, like I do. She has gone out with some real creeps, and when she doesn't get in by a decent hour I get worried about her."

"What do you do?" Betty asked.

"I just wait up for her until she gets home. The other night she didn't come home until 4 a.m., and I was about ready to call the cops. The man she was out with that night was someone I'd never seen before."

"Has she always gone out with men like that?" Mark asked.

"No, she didn't go out at all the first three years after the divorce. I think she thought my father would eventually come home. But he got married six months ago, and ever since that time she's gone out with any man who asks her. I've tried to talk some sense into her head and warn her about some of the men out there, but she doesn't seem to hear me."

"What are you going to do?" Amy inquired.

"There's nothing that I can do, except wait up for her and hope she gets home."

''That's what my mom does when I'm out on a date,'' Molly volunteered.

''Yeah, the roles are a little reversed, aren't they?'' Barry acknowledged. ''The ironic thing is that mom still wants to know where I'm going, who I'm going with, and what time I'll be home. I just wish she would show the same consideration she expects from me.''

''Consideration. Since when do the kids of divorced parents get any of that?'' These angry words came from Lydia. It was only two weeks since she'd told the class her parents were divorcing, and she and her mother would be moving out of the city.

''Are you still moving, Lydia?'' Jerry asked.

''Just as soon as the house sells. Mother wants to move close to our relatives since we'll be living alone. It doesn't seem to matter to either dad or mom that I don't want to change schools during my junior year. They're so caught up in their own problems that consideration for anyone else is out of the question.''

''It gets better, Lydia. It really does,'' Matt spoke in his normal calm, self-assured voice.

''How?'' Asked Lydia. ''Or maybe I should say, 'when'?''

''It doesn't usually come quickly, but it definitely does get better with time,'' Matt assured.

''How are things better for you?'' Lydia continued to question.

''Dad and I are understanding each other now. We've become friends, and that's a lot different from the way it was eight years ago when he moved out.''

''Would you like to tell us about it?'' Jan asked.

''For the most part, my father was available only to send

money, though my two brothers and I were required to spend the week-ends with him. He had girl friends over, and he didn't want to spend time with us. He didn't even want to see us. His girl friends were more important to him, and it was awful to be there. That went on for a long time, and then I just stopped going over to see him.

"When I was in about the fourth or fifth grade, I got to know Bob Tridell, our school custodian, and he became a good friend. At recesses and after school, I would help him clean up the campus. Soon he started allowing me to help him work on minor repairs around the school. Before long, I came to be known on campus as Mr. Tridell's helper. That made me feel really proud and happy. I felt needed and wanted.

"When I moved on to the junior high, I made friends with a boy my age, and then I became friends with his father and spent many, many hours at their house. By then dad had moved out of town, and my friend's father became a substitute father for me.

"Recently, my dad has moved back to town, and I've gotten to know and like him. I even had a dream last week about my parents.

"In the dream there was a white house that belonged to me. When my mother grew old and needed a place to live, I allowed her to live in this house—I didn't live there myself. And after a time, my father too needed a place, so I allowed him to move in with her. I left them to work out whatever needed to be worked out between them.

"I was later told by my therapist that the architecture in a dream frequently represents the dreamer, so this dream was me coming to terms inside myself with my father and mother. And not even with my father and mother now, but with what they were to me when I was young.

''This was particularly significant to me because for many years I was caught in the horrible game of playing one parent against the other. There was horrendous anger on my mother's part, and I conveyed that to my father. My mother filled me with fears and anger toward him by trying to convince me he was a horrible person, or that he was doing bad things. And, yes, my father was doing bad things, and yes, he wasn't available, but I wasn't allowed to figure out, for myself, who my dad was to me. As a result, I didn't feel comfortable with my father. There was a lot of pain.''

''But you said things are better now,'' Connie reminded him.

''Yes, they're much better. My father and I talked recently, and he admitted that all he was able to give me earlier was financial help. He said money was the only thing he was able to give because of the emotional stress he was going through. Now that's changed; he's grown emotionally, and he has more to give. Before, he couldn't give something he didn't have, but I didn't understand that at the time. I really like my father now.''

''Do you like your mother, also?'' Mary asked.

''Yes, I've always been close to my mother. My older brother was close to our father, but I was the one who my mother always called on when she needed help.''

''Since neither your father nor your mother has ever remarried, do you hope some day they'll get back together?'' Ben asked.

''No, not really. I think I've learned a few things through all of this, and one of those is that children of divorce don't need to take care of their parents. They shouldn't try to work out their parents' problems. If they do and they aren't successful, then the children are stuck with more guilt. And, anyway, it was probably out of our hands from the beginning.

"I've also learned that the whole situation is probably more upsetting to the child than to either of the parents."

Susan said, "As peer counselors trying to help our friends who are going through a family divorce, what's the one most important thing, in your opinion, we need to suggest to them?"

"I believe each person needs to find some neutral ground where he or she can talk about feelings. For me, peer counseling has been such a place during the past two years. It's been a class where I can talk about both of my parents without feeling like I'm going to be attacked by my mother trying to convince me my father's a bad person, or by my father trying to justify his behavior.

"Peer counseling has been a place where I could feel O.K. with my pain. I stopped crying for many, many years, but lately, I've learned to cry again."

"Do you think now you've resolved the divorce in your own mind?" John asked.

"I don't know if I have or not, but I'm happy. I'm getting along with both parents. I don't know if there is ever a total resolution. But like that dream, maybe I'm bringing things together in myself."

The bell sounded but members of the class lingered momentarily to talk individually with the students who had shared their feelings.

The following day, Kenneth Russ from Lake Family Services joined our class. Having a professional family therapist meet with the class two days during our discussion of family relationships was a practice that had proven very beneficial. I always chose speakers who related well to teenagers and who were in a position to give a few hours of community service, at no charge. Mr. Russ was always one of the most popular speakers. After a short presentation, he jumped right into current issues.

''Let's talk about how to handle a situation where dad expects you to spend the Christmas holidays with him—it's his turn to have you—but you feel guilty leaving mom to spend the day all alone. Do any of you have a problem similar to this?''

Tom had not raised his hand but had a comment, ''My problem is more complex than that. Dad wants to take me to Colorado on a two week skiing vacation, but mom would be left alone for the entire time. This is one of the bad things about being an only child. When I'm not at home, mom has no one. I don't want her to be unhappy at Christmas, but I'd really enjoy that trip.''

''You and your family go skiing every year during the holiday break, don't you?'' Steve asked.

''Yes, that's why it is so difficult this year. All three of us enjoy skiing, and this will be the first year that mom will not be going. Sometimes I think I should stay at home with her because it will seem so cruel to leave her; but then I think of the lodge and the ski slopes, and I can't imagine turning down the opportunity to go. Maybe I'm just selfish.''

Mr. Russ asked, ''Have you expressed your concerns about this matter to your dad and mom?''

''No, I haven't really talked to either one of them. Dad just said on the telephone last evening that he'd like to take me, and I told him I'd think about it. I haven't mentioned it to mom yet.''

''Let's do some role-playing,'' suggested Mr. Russ. ''I'll

play the part of your father and you be yourself. After we finish, we'll ask one of the young ladies in the class to play the part of your mother. By practicing this among friends, you may find it easier to sit down and talk openly and honestly to each of your parents."

Two things were accomplished by the role-playing exercise. Tom was gaining confidence in communicating his feelings to his parents, and the class was having an opportunity to review and refine the skills they had learned in earlier units.

After Tom had completed the role-playing, and suggestions had been given by Mr. Russ and the students, the other four students who had raised their hands were asked if they would like to role-play their situations. Sometimes students find it easier to share their problems in this type of activity than in an "I feel" session. Having two people sitting in chairs in the middle of the circle, communicating only with each other, seems to give the shy person the confidence he or she needs.

Two of the students wanted to role-play; the other two chose not to, and that was O.K. Pressure is never applied to get students to join in activities they don't feel comfortable doing. The time will come at a later date when they will be at ease with an exercise and join in.

The following day Tom bounced into class with a wide smile on his face. No one had to ask if he had been successful in talking to his father and mother.

"It worked. What a relief. That worry is off my mind," he informed the class as soon as the bell rang.

"Well, tell us about it," Mr. Russ said.

"I went home yesterday and told my mother that I needed to talk to her. I told her about the telephone call from dad and how I felt about leaving her at Christmas time. Being completely honest was very important to me, so I told her how much I would really like to go.

''She told me she already had been thinking about how we would handle the holidays, and she thought that dad would probably invite me to go with him. With this in mind, she called my grandparents and invited them to spend their winter vacation with her this year instead of going on their usual trip to Florida. From what she said, they were very happy to do that, so now she won't be alone.''

''That's great, Tom,'' Debbie said. ''I'm so glad it's worked out for you.''

''The neat thing about it is that I talked to mom and shared my feelings, and now I don't have to worry about it anymore. I called dad and told him why I'd hesitated in accepting his invitation, and he said he was proud of me for being concerned about mom. Everything couldn't have come out better.''

Mr. Russ spoke, ''Divorce always carries a lot of pain, and there are no easy answers to the problems it creates for the children in the family. But if you can just remember to keep talking—to your peers, to your mother, father, sisters, brothers—then dealing with it will be easier. Being alone with no one to talk to is the worst thing that can happen to you.''

With peer counseling available, students will always have someone nearby who is ready to listen.

CHAPTER TWELVE

Support—The Imprint of One Man

Dr. William Leonhardt, the county superintendent of schools, entered the peer counseling class, found a chair, and immediately seemed at home in the circle. To have a man of his importance in class might cause concern with some students, but not with this group. With his openness, honesty and warmth, he was able to establish rapport rapidly with the students. He seemed to understand exactly what the class was all about and was able to contribute—with his intelligence, wit, and enthusiasm—to the energy in the room.

As I sat and observed this tall, handsomely-greying man, I could not help but feel admiration for a person who would take the time from his busy day to travel to our school to observe this class. He had been asked to give the welcome address at the first California Peer Counseling Conference and wanted to see a class in action before his presentation.

The students spoke of why they had chosen the class and

shared their expectations. They demonstrated their skills through role-playing and other activities. Dr. Leonhardt asked questions, and they answered. The integrity of the class came through, and our visitor noticed. When the bell sounded, the students said good-bye to a new friend. A mutual respect had been established, and neither the superintendent nor the students would forget this day.

A few days later a letter arrived from Dr. Leonhardt expressing his feelings about the class. He wrote, ''I was very impressed with the caring and insights displayed by the young people in their acceptance of the responsibility to support each other.'' He went on then to add, ''It is obvious to me that the academic value of your class is lifelong!''

Two months later, Dr. Leonhardt wrote about peer counseling in the Superintendent's Corner of a news periodical. His article read:

''I can remember times as a teacher, principal, and father that not only couldn't I understand some of the feelings of young people, I had trouble understanding their language. The creation of a specialized lexicon of code words seems as much a part of growing up as trying new hair styles. Any attempt to interpret this lingo by those out of the age group is usually as successful as getting the bedroom cleaned regularly.

''In defense of the kids, I suspect the only thing harder than trying to bring up a child successfully these days is being the child. It has got to be in a world filled with today's distractions, peculiar role models, and ease of mobility. For my part, I think I see more attention being placed on the difficulties young people are forced to weather. The focus on issues such as child molestation, abuse, drugs and alcohol, abductions, and teenage suicide seems to be more concentrated than I can recall.

"Or maybe it's because we're trying to do something more constructive about these problems than sheltering our kids from them. There's a risk, of course, in openly discussing the distasteful. It can raise more questions or cause more anxiety than a particular situation may warrant. But on the whole, I think such openness has led to innovative ideas for helping our youngsters come through the turbulence of childhood and adolescence with little more than ruffled feathers.

"Let me share one example that I believe may point us in a direction for successfully helping young people in the future.

"This year, the office of Education became a major co-sponsor of the first statewide peer counseling conference held in California. I was invited to attend and, wanting to be somewhat informed on the process, visited a school in our county that has been using peer counseling for several years.

"What is peer counseling?

"Quite simply, it is using young people to help other people through personal or school problems. But not just by sitting in aimless 'rap sessions' and killing time telling stories. Peer counselors—at this school—are taught to be good listeners and supporters. They are taught these skills during classes that last about one quarter of the school year.

"For the rest of the year, they spend the class periods using their abilities to help each other through personal problems and conflicts at school. All conversation is considered confidential within the confines of the class.

"Teachers supervise, but do not interfere. The support comes from the young person's peers who listen, respond, listen some more, offer options, and, in general, try to let the student come to the best conclusion the best possible way—through personal decision making.

"It seemed to me that not only were the young people in that

class able to deal with many of the personal problems that could later surface as drug problems or suicides, but that the tone of the entire campus seemed different. I detected a feeling of openness and honesty, as well as less of the 'us versus them' attitude typically found between students and teachers.

''I think there is a message offered by peer counseling. The message is that as the world gets increasingly complicated—which it will—adults may become less and less equipped to deal with the complex feelings of young people as they grow up. Peer counseling suggests that in some cases it may be a good idea for adults to admit they are overwhelmed, not feel guilty about it, and find other ways of helping. In this case—and in many others—that help could come in the form of helping kids help other kids.

''After all, they do speak the same language.''

Yes, Dr. Leonhardt does understand about peer counseling. He had seen in one hour what had eluded others in many visits.

Because of the impression he had made with the students, they suggested to their peers that he be asked to give the baccalaureate address that year. The commencement committee agreed and an invitation was extended. They were delighted when he accepted the invitation. It wasn't until the day of the service that I found out his own son's baccalaureate was going on at the same time at another school. The dedication of this man to serve students was unquestionable.

Weeks before the baccalaureate, Dr. Leonhardt's secretary called and asked if the peer counselors would each send him an essay of one page or less telling how peer counseling had been beneficial to them or how it had enabled them to help someone else. They were happy to do this.

On the day of baccalaureate, the reason for his request became apparent. He spoke in glowing terms of our school—a place where students were concerned about each other and where a program was available to foster this concern. He talked about his previous visit to our campus and how impressed he was with the caring attitude he found in the peer counseling class. He issued a challenge to the students to remember what the peer counseling classes had contributed to the entire campus and to take the listening skills, the caring, and the concern for their fellowman with them as they left the familiar halls of their high school. He closed his address by reading excerpts from some of the essays the students had sent to him.

Portions from a few of these excerpts are as follows:

From a tenth grade student living alone with her mother:

''Peer counseling is an interesting class. It has taught me many things. It has helped me, and through me it has helped others.

''Peer counseling has taught me how to talk with other people more easily. I can now communicate better with my mother. By being able to talk with her, I have gained a better understanding of her point of view, and also why she makes decisions the way she does. As a result of this understanding, I don't argue with her about her decisions as much as I did.

''It has enabled me to feel at ease around other people whom I don't know well. I now feel comfortable going to parties or other places where I don't know everyone.

''Taking peer counseling has also helped me make a career decision. I have decided to go into counseling, and had it not been for this class I would not have been exposed to the counseling field and how much help it can be and how much good it can do.''

Another tenth grade girl wrote a poem:

''Peer counseling is a class but it's mostly a friendship.
And, as are all friendships, peer counseling is a learning experience.
In peer counseling not only do we give of ourselves, but we also learn how to give with the best results.
We don't learn for the sake of learning in such a class,
We learn for the sake of knowledge.
But most meaningfully, we learn for the sake of others.
And we'll never forget what we've learned.
Some choose to believe we use no textbooks,
But what better textbooks can we use than those of our lives and experiences?
Other classes might read what is written,
But the people of this class discuss what has been experienced.
Who would dare expect such of a textbook?
Some choose to believe we have no homework,
But when the lesson is life, what homework is better than life itself?
Our class is different than others,
Our class is a class of help, a class of kindness, and most of all
A class of pure and simple care.
The caring, the kindness and the desire to help are the prerequisites,
The true help comes with the knowledge of method,
For the ''how'' is all anyone must learn.
If the caring and desire to serve do not exist,
Then the ''how'' won't even be sought.
Our class cares, that's why there is a class,
For what greater gift can we give?
The class gives of itself to us,
And there is nothing more we can ask.

And through this giving amongst ourselves,
We learn how to give to others,
And we try to give our best.
Our class has learned a bit of wisdom:
It is in giving that we receive,
And every day we receive more and more.
Yes, peer counseling is a friendship full of love and caring, kindness, and sharing,
But most of all,
It is a friendship with life.''

A ninth grade boy wrote:

''A peer counselor is one who helps others. Yet, for myself being a peer counselor has meant helping me. I began this year of school scared and unsure of myself. It was a very rough time for me. My parents were just separated—something that wasn't supposed to happen in my family—and it was the beginning of a new life at high school. I often think what would have happened if I had not become a peer counselor. But I did and it has changed my life. It sounds like a lot but it is the truth. I am now standing on my own two feet, ready to walk.

''Being a peer counselor has helped me greatly with family problems. It has become a source of strength and hope. Second period has become my second family. Those in the class know me and accept me for what I am, not what I should be. I have learned to trust others and my own feelings with them. Sometimes I don't even do well with my mom. But with the knowledge gained in class, I can work towards expressing my emotions to others.

''I will make no claim that peer counseling is the answer to everything, but it is as close as anything has come yet. This then is what peer counseling has meant to me: Learning about myself so that I can help others to do the same.''

An eleventh grade girl wrote:

''My mother died when I was twelve years old. The trauma made me turn to sex and drugs. The experience and the way it was resolved has enabled me to help many others. In the past I had been giving advice to those seeking help from me. But in peer counseling I learned that I was wrong. Giving advice is not the way to help. Now I am more self-confident about how to help many others.

''Many others besides myself have not had parents at home to teach us of life and how to live it. High school cannot teach just academic skills because suicide, drugs, teenage sex, and dealing with death and many other things are not academics, but a great emotional part of life.''

From an eleventh grade boy:

''I don't really know where or how to start. I know that I'm really glad I took the class because it has taught me patience and understanding. Before I took peer counseling, I was constantly blowing up. I had the worst temper. Peer counseling has taught me how to keep calmer, not to fight, and to talk things out.

''I've never been the type to open up in front of a class before. I don't know why. I guess I'm just hard-headed. Now I'm not as scared to let my feelings be known. The class has made me more confident.''

A twelfth grade boy wrote:

''There are a lot of things I could say about the program, and they are all good. Without this program, I and several others would not be graduating. This may also be true with future peer counselors. Peer counseling is that important to me—it made me sit up and take notice of what I was doing.''

Words from a twelfth grade girl:

"Peer counseling was a unique experience that I wish could be shared by all. There are many vivid memories that I have of this class. Most of all, I remember all the close talks I've had. Those conversations were wonderful, and I'll never forget them. The people who I've peer counseled will forever stay close to me in my heart."

Another senior girl wrote:

"I've helped a person who was my own sister, who had a very bad problem with school. She never wanted to go, and all she did was party.

"As soon as I found out, I started talking to her about her problem. I was a very good active listener. I did not condemn her. I just listened to what she had to say about the entire situation, which nearly made me ill at times to hear. I asked questions when I did not understand, and at one point I asked her how she would feel about seeing a therapist. She flatly refused. So I continued to listen.

"She said she would be able to stop her behavior on her own free will, which I did not believe at the time. But I think by my talking to her, she started to realize how she really was messing up her life. She changed it completely.

"This was last year sometime, and now I'm happy to say she's a born again Christian, and her work in school is excellent. She said to me just a few months ago, 'Without you and your peer counseling skills, I would never have made it.' That made me feel good when she said that. I'm glad I had been trained to help."

Finally, from a senior boy:

"Peer counseling has given me many skills in which I am able to communicate and deal with all kinds of people and their problems. One situation in which I helped another was when this person was

about to commit suicide.

"He would drop hints every once in a while that would tell me he had this problem. I finally caught on and talked it out with him. I feel I helped him a lot, and I gave him a reason to stay alive. I am glad I caught on to these hints and talked it over with him because this person was my brother. If it weren't for peer counseling, I don't know how I would have handled that situation."

When Dr. Leonhardt finished his address, he received a standing ovation. As the audience continued their enthusiastic applause, I realized that mine was meant not only for the speech that I had just heard; but, also, for the man who delivered it. I clapped even harder as I looked at this highly-trained, academic person who related in such a humanistic way to the needs of students. He had a clear understanding of the peer counseling program—and also the courage to stand in an auditorium filled with parents, administrators, teachers, and students and proclaim the merits of a course that benefited young people so greatly.

Watching the senior class continue to stand and cheer, I knew that this baccalaureate would not be forgotten. Neither would this class ever forget the county superintendent who had missed his own son's program in order to contribute to theirs.

CHAPTER THIRTEEN

Graduation— The Journey Continues

"Look! I did it." The cheerful words came from a slim-figured girl standing inside the circle, slowly pirouetting so members of the group could see for themselves.

"You look terrific, Sally. You really do," Helen spoke with admiration in her voice.

Sally returned to her place in the circle, sat down, and continued her "I feel".

"The results you see started in our peer counseling class. With your friendship, love, and encouragement, I began to feel good about myself as a human being. And once that happened, then I could work on my weight. It took a while, but it was worth it. I feel terrific now!"

These students were not sitting in their familiar peer counseling circle on the high school campus. Those days were behind most of them. On this occasion they were seated in the spacious living room of a peer counseling alumnus. It was four days before Christmas and the college students had returned home for the holidays.

How easy it was for these young people to form a circle on the floor and pick up right where they had left off six months earlier. The fact that most of them had already completed one semester of college while some were still in high school was irrelevant. The closeness they had felt previously still remained. A magic permeated the air. Warmth, understanding, and love were so apparent they could almost be plucked from the atmosphere.

"Hey, Sally, whatever happened to your boyfriend, Hank?" Angela asked.

"I got rid of him," Sally responded without hesitation.

Lucy screamed, "Y-e-a" and began clapping her hands. The applause spread around the circle.

"Good for you," Ruby rejoiced. "I never felt he was right for you."

"Yeah, remember how we had reservations about him all last year," Julie added.

"I didn't understand why you were so concerned," Sally confessed, "But I do now. He was kind of a creep, wasn't he?" she laughingly added.

"It wasn't so much that he was a creep as it was that you deserved better," Jack offered.

"After I lost weight I, too, began to see that I deserved better." Sally confided. "Before, I didn't feel I deserved anything—not even a creepy boyfriend."

The lively conversation continued around the circle as each person shared his "I feel". When it came to Robert's turn to talk, the mood changed. The somberness of his opening statement cast a quietness over the merriment of the group.

"I really need to tell you about my first semester," Robert began. "I haven't felt I could talk to anyone at school. And I haven't had the courage to tell my parents yet. Maybe after I get this off my chest tonight, I can tell them."

Robert was a top student in his high school class. What could have happened his first semester in college to cause him the anxiety we saw on his face tonight?

"Sounds serious," Jeff said.

"It's about as serious as it can get," Robert responded.

"We're listening," Sally informed.

Robert continued, "I left high school feeling confident, self-assured, and, yes,—maybe a little cocky. Being accepted by one of the best engineering schools in the country was my dream come true."

"I remember how happy you were when you got your acceptance letter," John added.

"Well that happiness didn't last very long after I arrived at college. I knew in a matter of weeks that I was in real trouble. I had never seen so many 'brains' in my life—and on top of that, they studied night and day."

"But you have brain power too," Ginny added.

"I thought so until I came up against those students, and I realized that I didn't have the intellectual curiosity or the desire I saw in my classmates.

"All of a sudden, instead of being top dog in a class, I was low man on the totem pole. I'm afraid I didn't make the adjustment well. Instead of studying harder and bringing my grades up, I retreated within myself. God, did I need you people to talk to."

"There wasn't a peer counseling class on campus?" Jack asked.

"No, if there had been, I'm confident I wouldn't be in

the trouble I'm in now. I would have given anything to have a group like this to sit down with and unload on. I needed support—I needed it badly.''

''What happened when you didn't get it?'' Mary asked.

''I fell apart. I lost my confidence, pride, ambition. The word 'loneliness' took on a new meaning to me. I'm afraid I'm in sad shape. The grades haven't arrived yet, but I'm not expecting to pass more than two of my courses. That will mean I'll be on probation, and if I don't bring my grades up next semester I will be out!''

''Do you want to go back?'' Steve asked.

''Last semester all I could think of was getting away from there, but now I'm away—and I realize I do want to go back. Somehow I have to gain back my self-confidence and my determination to succeed. When I found myself in a place where everyone was just as smart as I was, or more so, it blew me away. I wasn't used to that kind of competition, and I couldn't talk out my frustrations.''

''Robert, I found I missed the support of the peer counselors too, so I decided to form a support group on campus,'' Gary informed. ''I found that I was not alone in needing this; we were all away from home, living in the dorms, competing in a more difficult arena.''

''You organized this yourself?'' Robert asked.

''Yes, organizing it wasn't difficult. The hard part was having the mental energy necessary to be an effective leader in such an emotionally charged group.''

''Sounds exciting,'' Robert responded. ''I'd like to talk to you about that more before I go back to school.''

''Fine, anytime,'' Gary volunteered. ''But do go on with your 'I feel.'''

Robert continued. He had the attention of friends who

cared about him and were eager to help him regain his confidence. He felt secure and loved in this group, and he poured out all the frustration and pain of the previous months.

Going around the circle until everyone had expressed his or her "I feel" lasted into the night. But the benefits of the reunion were immeasurable. There was a bond within this group that would live on no matter how great a distance the students were separated.

Reunions were only one way of getting together after graduation. There were other ways as well.

The telephone. That wonderful instrument used so frequently during high-school-years had not been forgotten.

I received calls from all over the country. There were the information seeking calls, "Hi, Mrs. Sturkie. How are you? How is peer counseling? Bet the group you have now isn't as good as our group. By the way, have you heard from anyone lately? Bring me up to date on what's going on."

Then there were the what-do-I-do-next calls.

Carmen—you remember her, the senior class president—called me from a college in Northern California.

"Mrs. Sturkie, please listen and see if I have covered all the bases. I don't want to overlook anything. This girl in our dorm has been acting very strangely, like locking herself in her room, getting angry, lashing out at anyone who happens to be near her. She has started to confide in me a little, and I'm picking up on a few things that lead me to believe she is on the verge of suicide. I've already done this... and this...and this. Have I forgotten anything?"

Then there were the recommendation calls, "Hey, Mrs. Sturkie, remember when you said that peer counseling would open doors for us if we ever wanted to be a resident assistant in the dorm? Well, would you believe, you were right! I have been selected over five other girls, but the director needs a letter from you.''

And then the summer camp counselor recommendation requests, ''Mrs. Sturkie, I have a terrific opportunity to work this summer as a camp counselor. They said they need somebody like me who has been trained to listen. And they need a recommendation from you. Don't forget to tell them all my good points. You do remember them, don't you?''

Letters. From all over the United States and abroad. You remember Olga who had the lead in ''The King and I''. She wrote:

''Dear Mrs. Sturkie,

''If you only knew how much I miss you and all the others.

''I wish so much I could be with all of you this semester and sit in the circle as I used to. I miss that fellowship so much.

''Well, I'm back home in Norway. People are telling me this is home and it's here where I'm supposed to feel that I belong. But after being in America for a year as an exchange student I feel like I belong there too. My feelings say that I belong in Brownsboro, but my common sense says that I belong here. Is that strange? I think so.

''I'm back in school again, but I miss so many things that I had last year. Do the students there know how lucky they are to have peer counseling? I'm so grateful I learned the skills.

''Peer counseling has added something in my life that will always be there. Really, I'm serious. I think I had it in me before, but peer counseling was the door for letting it all out. I'm so grateful. It is such a good class.

''I would like to get peer counseling started in my school.

''I plan to contact the psychology teacher and explain the concept of the class to him. I need your help though. Please tell me the proper way to go about getting the class started. We need it here in the same way the students need it in the United States.

''Please take care and send my love to all the peer counselors.

Love,
Olga''

And Olga was not alone in spreading peer counseling.

Julia was a junior when her father was transferred to another state. A year passed before I heard from her. I opened her letter quickly and read:

''Dear Mrs. Sturkie,

''Bet you thought I'd forgotten about you and peer counseling.

''Well, I haven't. I'm just not much of a writer. Remember my short journals?

''Anyway, I've got such good news that I just had to let you know.

''Due to my efforts—yes, I'm proud to take credit for it—we now have peer counseling at my new school. Only one class, but it is our first semester to have it.

''I will graduate in a few weeks, but I'm happy to leave something behind for the kids next year and the years to come—peer counseling.

''Thought you'd like to know.

Love ya,
Julie''

Besides helping to start peer counseling classes, others worked in jobs which required the use of their peer counseling skills.

Remember Felicia? I received an invitation to an open house for a new eating disorders unit in a local hospital. I attended the event to show support for Felicia. She was working in this counseling setting while still attending college. Just the type of place I would expect her to work.

And Mary? With two and one-half years of sobriety, she is working at a drug rehabilitation center— again, a peer counselor working in a counseling setting while attending college.

The alumni of the peer counseling classes are spread in many different states and countries. But wherever they are, they seem to remember the phrase they heard on the last day of class, "Once a Peer Counselor, Always a Peer Counselor."

They will be peer counselors while in colleges, at drug abuse centers, in eating disorder care units, at summer camps, in college dorms.

In years to come they will continue to use their skills. They will be better husbands and better wives because they will know that good communication is the key to healthy relationships. They will be caring parents because they have learned the value of being good listeners. They will be community leaders because they have learned to reach out to others. They will make better employees and better employers because they will be able to communicate their needs rather than stew in their own frustrations. They will be good neighbors because they have learned to be nonjudgmental and accepting of peoples of different races, customs, creeds, appearances, and beliefs.

As they complete their studies and enter their professions, the world will have more doctors who really listen to their patients, more teachers who are concerned with the total needs of the students, more engineers who strive to develop technology that enriches and enhances the quality of life for everyone.

The list could go on and on— because remember:

ONCE A PEER COUNSELOR, ALWAYS A PEER COUNSELOR.

Get ready, world. They are on their way.

PART III

How to Start a Peer Counseling Program

The room was filled with the dignitaries of the city. The chief of police sat next to the city manager. Three school board members sat clustered together, facing another colleague across the aisle. The city council members were dispersed throughout the room, one talking to the PTA council president and another engaged in conversation with the executive manager of the chamber of commerce.

As the speaker was introduced, a quiet came over the room. These people had come together on a warm September evening in a united effort to evaluate a drug abuse program for their city that would educate the public, rehabilitate drug users, and prevent drug abuse.

Dr. Larry Lewis, well-known drug abuse therapist, was speaking, ''Kids get other kids started in using drugs, and kids should be used to help get kids off drugs. They listen to each other. Peer counseling helps kids with drug abuse problems.''

How gratifying it was to sit in an audience of city and school leaders and hear those words spoken. He went on to say, ''The success rate of adolescents who have participated in an inpatient hospital program staying off drugs is only 35%, but the rate increases to 85% if the adolescent has been in a program that involves peer counselors.''

To sit quietly in my chair and not jump up and cheer took a Herculean effort. The same tremendously positive power I had seen generated in the peer counseling class was now being proclaimed by experts in the field of drug abuse. I sensed a new era for peer counseling—a time of tremendous growth, of more programs being available in schools and colleges, drug abuse facilities, senior citizen centers, police academies, planned parenthood clinics, churches, camps—any place where peers can be trained to help peers.

Because of this growing interest in peer counseling, the question I'm most frequently asked is: ''How can I get a peer counseling class started in my school?'' While there are many different ways to do it, I have broken the process into the six basic steps I've found to be essential in setting up a successful program.

STEP ONE: SELLING THE PROGRAM.

Selling the administration and the school board on the need for this program in your school is the first step. Because peer counseling is not as familiar as math or English, you may need to educate the educators. If a neighboring school has a program, ask the teacher of that program if you and someone else from your school may visit. Then invite one of your administrators or school board members to join you in observing the class. Taking one of these people with you may save you hours later on, because once an administrator or a school board member is impressed with the program, he or she will sell it to the others.

Since school board members are very cost-conscious, it is wise to point out how peer counseling will save the district money. Peer counseling helps the school budget in the following ways:

- Peer counselors work with students having truancy problems. Because a truant may dislike a school where he feels no one cares, having a peer counselor pay attention to potential truants may keep him or her coming to classes. Therefore, average daily attendance will go up, resulting in the district receiving more money.
- Potential high school dropouts often stay in school through the work of peer counselors. Therefore, the loss in revenue to the school district from having fewer students does not occur.
- Vandalism is decreased through positive peer pressure, thus saving the district costly maintenance repairs. When a rebellious student finds someone at school who he feels cares, understands, and accepts him, some of his anger may dissipate and he will not feel a need to act out his hostility in a destructive way.
- The school's overall grade point average often increases due to peer tutoring. The reputation of the school is enhanced; thus making the community a more popular place to live. As people with children move into a popular district, the revenue from taxes increases, which in turn provides more money for the schools.
- Using peer counselors can increase the effectiveness of the counseling department without hiring additional counselors. The students can become extended hands of

the counselors and provide services that can free the professionals to take care of other demands, such as academic and college counseling.

Aside from the financial benefits, you will also want to point out to the school board that having peer counselors on campus assists in drug abuse programs, new student orientation, academic tutoring, suicide prevention, college and career planning and so on—the list is endless.

If your board is impressed by statistics, you might quote a study done by the Pajaro Valley Unified School District. This district implemented a program called Project H.O.L.D. (Help Overcome Learner Dropouts), using peer counselors to help keep kids in school. Two matched groups of potential dropouts were targeted. One group was helped by peer counselors, the other was not. Their attendance and dropout rates were compared. The findings were impressive:

- DROPOUTS—After three years 72% of those potential dropouts helped by peer counselors were still enrolled in the districts while only 22% of the other targeted group were still enrolled.

- TRUANTS—More than half of the chronic truants (20 or more days absent the preceding year) who were being helped by peer counselors had no unexcused absences in the third year of the study.

- CREDITS—Forty-five students who had less than 20 units of credit each increased that credit by 66% with the help of peer counselors. The comparison students who got no help from peer counselors gained only 5%.

STEP TWO: SELECTING THE RIGHT TEACHER.

After the school board approves your proposal for the course, the next important step is selecting the teacher.

Although the selection is made by the administration and approved by the school board, suggestions certainly may be offered by others who are concerned.

If the old adage is true that any class is made or broken by the teacher, then it is doubly true for a peer counseling class. I've seen successful programs fold when a new teacher took over. And the irony is that the unsuccessful teacher may have been extremely successful in teaching some other subject. Success in teaching other classes does not guarantee or even promise success in teaching peer counseling. No teacher should ever be forced to accept responsibility for teaching this course because having a great desire to teach this type of program is essential.

Successful peer counseling teachers know that the spotlight is not often on them. The students are the pivotal points of the class. The teachers do as much listening as they do talking. They manage the classes by creating respect rather than by being controlling. Much of the teaching is done by role-playing; therefore, the teachers need to be secure people who are comfortable with themselves. Sincerity is of the upmost importance. Students can spot a fake comment or see through any incongruity immediately.

Other characteristics to look for in a teacher for this important position are:

- a real caring spirit
- a desire to make a difference in students' lives
- patience (and more patience)
- the ability to respect confidentiality at all times and in all situations

- a high energy level
- tenacity to "hang in" with a student and not give up
- a respect by colleagues and students.

The teacher also needs to be someone who will reach out to the community and become acquainted with professionals from many different helping agencies. Inviting these experts to the class will allow your students to receive the most current information from different fields, as well as acquaint them with professional resources.

High school counselors are probably the best qualified to teach peer counseling because of the training they received to be credentialed. However, this may not always be true. A teacher who relates well to students, is empathetic and nonjudgmental, and is highly motivated to teach the class may be more effective than a counselor who is interested only in the academic progress of the students. In such a case, the teacher may seek assistance from the guidance counselors, the school psychologist, or interns from nearby graduate counseling programs.

Finally, before any person takes on the responsibility of a peer counseling class (no matter how well he or she may be prepared academically), he or she should visit classes in neighboring schools, attend workshops, and read available literature on the subject. The perceptive person will see quickly that teaching this class can be invigorating and rewarding.

STEP THREE: SELECTING THE STUDENTS.

It is imperative for a peer counseling class to have a cross-section of students; therefore, you will need to pre-select the first class. There are two reasons for this:

1. The students will return to their own circle of friends during lunch and after school and thereby spread peer counseling among all groups on campus.

2. Students will gain a new understanding of peers with whom they have never associated, and a greater tolerance and acceptance of the differences among people will develop from the class. This seems to carry on into life after graduation.

Before the beginning of the first semester, the person who has been designated to teach peer counseling should invite all prospective students to a meeting at noon or after school. During this time the teacher will explain the program and ask those students who are interested to put their name on a sign-up sheet. Since usually only one class will be taught during the first semester, selection of students will need to be based on interviews with a large number of students. It is preferable that two people do the interviewing. Each interviewer should see all of the students on an individual basis. This eliminates any question of favoritism and ensures a more accurate assessment of the students. Care should be taken to select students with a wide range of academic abilities. Campus leaders, students with attendence and discipline problems, athletes, cheerleaders, shy students, students representing all races on campus, foreign exchange students, handicapped individuals—all of these should come together in this class.

After the first class is chosen, there will never be a need to select the students again. They will each tell their friends; thereafter, a representation of all groups will sign up for the peer counseling classes.

Once the students are selected, parent consent letters should be signed and placed on file before the first class begins. In the consent letter the parents should be informed of the goals of the class and the material that will be presented. After the class has been in progress for a couple of weeks, an invitation should be extended to all parents to attend an evening meeting. I have found that the parents enjoy sitting in a circle like the students do. They should be given the opportunity to express their feelings and have their concerns addressed. This is also a good time to get parent volunteers to sign up to help with the ''shirting'' banquet at the end of the semester.

Explain to the parents at this meeting, the importance of the confidentiality contract each student has signed. Some parents may question why their teenager cannot relate to them what happens in the class. They are usually satisfied once they understand that without guidelines for confidentiality, students will not feel safe to share with each other and will not be able to model confidentiality when helping other students later outside the class.

At the completion of the first semester, the beginning peer counselors go on to an advanced peer counseling class. A new class of beginners should also start during the second semester, which means there will then be two classes on campus. The following year the program will probably grow to three or four classes. There should always be a beginning class and as many advanced classes as are necessary to meet the needs of the peer counselors.

STEP FOUR: STRUCTURING THE CLASS.

As stated in the foreword, schools may choose to structure peer counseling classes in different ways. Ideally, I believe, the class should be on par with any other class on campus. This means the class should meet on a daily basis, academic requirements should be set for completion with tests to be taken and credit to be given. The courses should appear on the student's transcript along with all of the other classes. This format is used in many schools and is proving very successful.

STEP FIVE: THE CURRICULUM.

During the first semester, the peer counseling student must develop his counseling skills, and learn how to use these skills in dealing with the problems teenagers face. These skills are presented in individual units. A sample curriculum for the first semester might be as follows:

Unit One: Developing Social Ease
Unit Two: Introduction to Active Listening
Unit Three: Sending Effective Messages
Unit Four: Values Clarification
Unit Five: Decision-Making
Unit Six: Developing Self-Awareness
Unit Seven: Developing Helping Skills
Unit Eight: School Related Problems
Unit Nine: Peer Pressure
Unit Ten: Family Problems
Unit Eleven: Sexuality
Unit Twelve: Drug Abuse
Unit Thirteen: Child Abuse
Unit Fourteen: Suicide
Unit Fifteen: Death and Dying

Throughout all units, students participate in various activities such as keeping weekly journals, doing book reports, hearing guest speakers, doing lessons, and sharing in "I feel" sessions. These activities are described in detail under Step 6.

While the students are developing their skills, they must

also be developing positive attitudes toward helping others. Students must never be allowed to disparage themselves or other students.

One of the most important things to remember in teaching a peer counseling class is to be flexible. For example, if a student on campus were killed in a car accident but you had not reached unit fifteen on death and dying, you should skip to that unit immediately and go back to the others later. Meeting the needs of the students when the situation calls for it should take priority over any schedule.

When the first semester is completed and the students become advanced peer counselors, their class is conducted on a daily basis as usual. The difference now is that the peer counselors may begin counseling other students outside of class. Potential concerns about helping students outside the group are addressed with the support the peer counselor receives from the advanced class. The new counselor may discuss any problems or any questions that may arise. To keep confidentality, the name of the counselee is never mentioned.

Advanced peer counselors should not be required to counsel other students. Only when the students feel ready do they begin working with others. Students are ready to take on this challenge at different times, and no one should expect that everyone will do so the day after graduating from the beginning class. The grade for advanced classes is not dependent on when the peer counselor begins counseling others or on the number of students he helps.

STEP SIX: CONDUCTING THE CLASS.

The teacher will face many challenges once the class gets underway. Here are some other hints and suggestions for jumping the hurdles of running the course.

Class Unity

Great effort should be exerted the first few weeks to "cement" the class into a whole. When you observe a feeling of trust among the students for one another, you will know this bond has been accomplished. It will be evidenced by a willingness to share very meaningful feelings during the "I feel" day. This exercise should be scheduled once a week. You may use any day of the week as the "I feel" day, but once that day has been set, it should be observed regularly. Students look forward to this time of sharing, and if a speaker, film, or any other activity was scheduled for that particular day the students may be upset.

Follow these guidelines to "cement" the class and develop a bond among students:

1. Spend as many class periods on Unit One as needed for the students to become acquainted.

The teacher may feel pushed to "get on with the lesson plans" and to skip lightly over the unit on developing social ease. Don't give in to this temptation. Don't rush into teaching active listening skills until each person in the class can introduce the other classmates and relate one fact about them each. This should not be difficult after a week of get-acquainted activities. Here are several examples that can be used:

- INTRODUCTION GAME: Put four chairs in the center circle, give the students a few minutes to talk to each other, and then let each one introduce the other three to the class, which observes and listens. This is repeated until everyone has been in the center circle.
- SPECIAL MEMORIES GAME: Ask each student to

bring something to class that has a special meaning to him or her (a photo, ring, book) and have the person share with the class why it is special. During this exercise one year, a foreign exchange student brought a picture of her father who died when she was three. In explaining to the class how important that picture was to her throughout the years, she revealed aspects of herself that touched everyone in ways they will always remember.

● BIRTHDAY GAME: Divide the class in groups according to birthday months. Allow the students time to communicate with the others in their group. When they return to the large circle, ask each group to share with the class what they had in common other than being born in the same month.

2. Develop an atmosphere of trust. If the teacher makes the students aware that trust is one of the most important elements in the class, and that she or he will not violate it, the students will soon model this behavior. Because students may have had negative experiences previously with not being able to trust adults, it is crucial that the teacher does not betray their trust.

3. Instill in each student the belief that he or she is important to the class, and when absent, he or she will be missed.

4. Designate "care groups" for everyone in the class. To form these groups, number the students off into groups of five, and have all of the number ones form one group, all the twos, another group, all the threes another group, etc. Members of the care groups are to be concerned about each other on a daily basis. Have them exchange phone numbers so they may call each other outside of class.

New Student Luncheon

After the students have developed and practiced being at ease socially by getting to know each other in class, assign them to a new student on the campus. Ask the class members to introduce themselves to the new students and invite them to a New Student Luncheon to be hosted by the peer counseling classes.

The purpose of this luncheon is to help not only new students feel at ease, but also to help the new peer counselors transfer the social skills they have just learned to a setting outside the classroom. This luncheon should take place sometime during the first month of school.

The peer counselors may bring potluck dishes from home. Committees should be formed to decorate, serve, and clean up. Make certain that all the administrators, including the superintendent and school board members, are invited. Members of the high school band may be asked to play during the meal. Don't forget to ask your local paper to cover the event.

The "I Feel" Day

Much has been said about the importance of this activity. In this exercise, the students share their feelings on an individual basis, with the other members of the class listening very attentively. Usually the students speak one by one going around the circle; however, if students choose not to share, they just say "pass," and the next person shares. Pressure should never be placed on anyone to share if they choose not to. They will speak when they are comfortable in the class and trust has been built. Select one day a week as an "I feel" day, and use the same day the following weeks.

When you first introduce this exercise you may explain

it to the students by asking them to complete the sentence, "I feel—." As the weeks progress, the "I feels" gain in length and seriousness. Sometimes they must be extended into the following day if a complex problem has been presented which takes up a great deal of time.

Discretion, Ethics, Confidentiality, and Liability

The teacher needs to make peer counselors aware that there are things they cannot and should not attempt to handle. The peer counselor should never be placed in a situation that is either life threatening to him or her or to the counselee. Never is the peer counselor to be involved in assisting a student in breaking the law.

The discretion of the student in certain matters is crucial. The students need to know that calling the teacher at home is appropriate whenever the student finds himself or herself in a situation he or she can't handle. The list of community resource people is available to the student, and previous guest speakers also seem to be open to having students call them if a crisis arises. Knowing where to look for help quickly should be learned in the beginning class.

The students need to know that the teacher will not violate their confidences as they will not violate each others. The teacher must make the students aware from the very beginning that he or she will report child abuse to the authorities, and will report any hints of suicide to the parent or guardian. Also, the students tell their counselees they will report such cases.

Liability is a word that makes school districts nervous, and it is something that is usually discussed before a peer counseling class is implemented. Peer counselors do not give advice; therefore, they do not tell students what to do. This fact decreases the chance of liability.

Confidentiality Contract

On the first day of each new semester, peer counselors sign forms stating they understand that everything said in class is to be confidential. The typed forms are short and to the point. The teacher makes certain the students understand exactly what they are signing. I have always found them to be very willing to sign the contract because they realize a confidential atmosphere is necessary if they are to trust and share.

Breaking Confidentiality

What happens when someone breaks the confidentiality contract?

This is certain to happen at some time, so be prepared for it in advance and don't panic. Usually the contract is broken unintentionally; nevertheless, it is a serious breach of trust and demands immediate attention.

If students have heard something that was shared confidentially in class talked about on campus, make sure that the person who first shared the information was not the one who told others outside the class. Of course, the person has every right to do this; and that may be, in fact, what has happened. If it has been a true breach of confidentiality and someone has reported it in class, a discussion should be held about the seriousness of this offense. If students feel what they say will be taken out of class, sharing will cease.

Should the teacher be given information privately about a breach of confidentiality, she or he may wish to talk with the individual who broke the contract and come to a resolution without bringing the matter to the attention of the entire class. This sometimes is preferable if the class is not aware of the incident at the onset.

When it is handled well by the teacher and the class, learning can take place even in an unfortunate situation, such as breaking a contract. I have never known a student to make a mistake of this nature twice, but if it does happen, serious consideration should be given to asking the student to leave the class. The students must feel they can trust their fellow peer counselors.

Discipline

The teacher should tell the students at the beginning of the semester exactly what conduct is expected of them in this class. After teaching the students the principles of appropriate helping behavior, the teacher then allows them to take responsibility and claim ownership for minor infractions of the rules. Of course, if a major incident such as a fight erupts, the teacher would certainly take charge. It is highly unlikely that a major problem would occur in a peer counseling class, however, and minor offenses can be dealt with by positive peer pressure.

For example, since listening is one of the skills learned in this class, practicing it is very important. If someone forgets and is talking when another person has the floor, anyone in the class may ask for quiet. This can be done by uttering a one word signal the class has previously designated, such as "support."

After visiting our class, one of our English teachers expressed amazement at how well-behaved Kenneth was. She stated that in her class she was constantly having to remind him to stop talking. Knowing that I did not have the reputation as being a strict disciplinarian, she wondered how I managed to have the class room behavior she witnessed. I told her that, first, the students claimed ownership for their own behavior; and, second, they felt a responsibility for the atmosphere of the entire class.

Even though there are always students in class who are known to have discipline problems, these students rarely create a disturbance in their peer counseling class. They seem to quickly adapt to the positive attitude of the other students and to the expectations of the teacher and the class.

Journals

Request the students to keep a journal in which they write their feelings about anything that happens in their lives during the week. They may write on something that has taken place in the classroom, at home, at work, or in extracurricular activities. The feelings may reflect happy or sad times. The emphasis is for the students to write whatever they want and to know they will not be judged negatively for any of their feelings. The journals are read only by the teacher. This rule is never violated. After they are read, they are returned to the student.

Having students turn in weekly journals serves four purposes:

1. Students learn to recognize and express their feelings.

2. Writing about feelings may serve as a catharsis for built-up anger, frustration, or hostility.

3. The student can participate in homework assignments without fear of failure. The journals are not given letter grades, only a check at the top of each page to signify the page was read. Spelling or punctuation is never corrected, no matter how tempting it may be to use the red pen. However, a weekly check is placed in the grade book for each journal report, and the students need to understand that missing journals will lower their grade in the class.

4. Teachers get to know the students extremely well by reading the journals. Sometimes a student may be very shy about sharing certain feelings in the "I feel" sessions but will welcome the opportunity to share or ask for help in a journal.

Notebooks

Encourage students to purchase an inexpensive vinyl three-ring notebook in which to keep all their peer counseling work. Using a section of their regular school notebook is not advisable, since peer counseling notebooks will be turned in quarterly to the teacher to be reviewed and graded. Also, their peer counseling work should be kept separate because it will become a valuable reference book to be used in future semesters.

The criteria that will be applied for the grading of the notebooks should be announced at the beginning of the class.

In the notebook should be placed the handout sheets relating to the activities done in class, notes and brochures from guest speakers, newspaper and magazine articles, reports given in class, weekly journals, lists of community resources, book reports, class goals and objectives.

Guest speakers

I found guest speakers to be invaluable and invited them to class frequently. Hearing an expert speak enables the students to receive the most current information relating to a given unit of study. Also, it allows the students the opportunity to ask questions of professionals regarding their chosen careers, thus expanding the range of potential career choices for the students.

Be bold and ask top professionals to speak to your class. The results are worth the effort. Having the best speakers possible, particularly noted representatives from community agencies, will prove beneficial in acquainting the students with the resources available to them and others.

The day following a speaker's visit, schedule time to answer any questions the students may have concerning what they heard the previous day. This discussion time also gives the teacher an opportunity to correct any misinterpretations the students may have. Students should be given the opportunity to evaluate each speaker, listing both pros and cons relating to preparation, knowledge of subject matter, and delivery. The teacher should keep the evaluations and refer to them when deciding if the speaker should be invited back in the future.

Teacher Committee

Form a committee of teachers on campus and meet with them periodically to answer questions and discuss concerns involving peer counselors. These teachers in turn will have knowledge of the program to give to their co-workers.

Banquets

A banquet should be held at the end of the first semester. The students will have completed their training in the basic skills, and the banquet ceremony is a celebration of this accomplishment. Having the students do the preparation for the event allows them to claim ownership of it and assures a well-attended, joyful occasion.

The high point of the banquet will be the "shirting" event where all counselors completing their first semester will receive a peer counseling sweatshirt. In wearing this shirt, they will announce their new status to the world and let others know they are people who can help.

The entire class should decide, by popular vote, on the color of the sweatshirt and the color of the lettering. After shirts are presented at the banquet, the students are then permitted to wear them on campus. To wear a peer counseling shirt is a real honor, and the students take this ''shirting'' ceremony seriously.

Weeks in advance, committees should be formed to prepare for the banquet. The group in charge of collecting money for the sweatshirts should be selected first. Another committee should be established to send invitations to parents, administrators, school board members, and other guests. Placing a form at the end of the invitation to be used as an R.S.V.P. will help in knowing how many tables to set up.

The school cafeteria, decorated with colorful paper streamers and table decorations, may serve as a place for the banquet. Food may be provided by the students in the form of a potluck dinner.

Certificates

When the students receive their shirts at the banquet, they should also receive a certificate stating they have completed training in developing peer counseling skills. This should be an attractive certificate signed by the teacher, the principal, and the superintendent. The students need to be told of the value of this recognition. They may present the certificate when they apply for work in summer camps, as resident assistants in college dormitories, or many other counseling positions.

Awards

As the teacher of the class, you may want to suggest to the students that they offer awards for outstanding peer counselors. Members of the class may want to present two seniors with an Outstanding Peer Counselor Award at the Seniors Awards Assembly. If so, the teacher may suggest that students take up a small collection and purchase plaques to present to the two outstanding peers. These students should be in the Advanced Peer Counseling class and be truly exemplary peer counselors. These coveted awards should be selected by popular vote of the class.

Community Resources

During the first semester, the students will need to spend several weeks investigating the community resources they will need to use for referrals during the following semesters. Students may each choose one agency to investigate and make an oral report to the class about the function of that agency, the hours of operation, the age level it serves, the address, telephone number, and cost. The other students should copy down this information and place it in their notebooks. Some students may wish to transfer it later to note cards and file them alphabetically in a small box.

Media Coverage

Many articles were published in the local newspapers about our program. We were well aware of the good PR this media coverage created.

One paper ran an article and a picture covering a luncheon for new students sponsored by the peer counselors. Shortly afterwards I found an immaculately dressed, stylishly coiffured, senior citizen waiting in the counseling office to see me.

"I read the article in the paper," she began after being seated in my office, "and I was so impressed with what this school does to welcome new students that I'm here to pick up an admission pack for my grandson. My son's family will be moving here from back East next week, and because of your peer counselors' efforts to make new students welcome, my son is going to buy a house in this city."

What better coverage could we ask for?

In fact, our peer counseling functions had been photographed and written up positively so many times in the newspapers that our first scrap book was already filled. Even the widely read LOS ANGELES TIMES had given us an extensive write-up.

Being in Southern Califonia, some of the movie production companies heard about our program and visited our school. These creative, sensitive people were captivated by the spirit of the class. After an initial visit, the director, producer, and writer from one well-known company asked if they might return and attend the shirting banquet. Invitations were extended and all three showed up for the event.

The good word must have spread because after their visit, we had visits from other companies. When a documentary was produced and released by Walt Disney Studios on the subject of date rape, the writer used our peer counseling class for the setting, and some of our own peer counselors were cast as extras in the film. Peter, one of the second year peer counselors, was elated when he was given a small speaking part.

Another production company, in conjunction with the Scott Newman Foundation, produced a one hour video on drug abuse prevention, and peer counseling was selected as one of the programs to be used in this film. When the writer asked for students to critique the script, the peer counselors gathered at my home during the Christmas holidays and gave helpful suggestions. Weeks later they were delighted to learn they would have the privilege of being the peer counseling class that appeared on the video. They donated their time and talents to this worthwhile project because they knew from experience on their own campus how important their program was in the prevention and intervention of drug abuse.

Other writers, producers, and directors visited, and they were equally impressed with the peer counselors and the program. There was even talk of a TV movie and then possibly a TV series.

Our program was recognized not only by the media, but by many other schools in Southern California as being a model program.

You may also invite newspaper reporters to your events involving the peer counselors, parents, teachers, and administrators. When the reporters and photographers arrive on your campus, take time to introduce yourself and to welcome them. If you have invited them to a New Student Luncheon or a Shirting Banquet, make sure they, too, are offered food. Let them know you appreciate their time and professionalism. When you have another event you would like covered by the media, inquire if it is possible for the same team to come again. If they do, a rapport may soon be established. Having your events covered by the press is then enjoyable for you and the peer counselors, as well as a welcome assignment for the reporters and photographers.

If your local television station has community service time available, you might inquire about having a program presented by the peer counselors. An example of this might be a presentation on drug abuse during National Drug Awareness month.

Four or five peer counselors may form a speaking team,

with your help. A presentation could be given to local service clubs, other public or private schools, and senior citizen centers. A program of peer counselors sharing some of their experiences was presented to a local Rotary Club. This led to the peer counselors being invited to other clubs in other cities. The peer counselors delighted in telling the good news of peer counseling, and the audience enjoyed an informative and entertaining program. These programs were often first announced in the local paper and later followed-up by an article and a picture.

Support comes from people who are aware of all the good things the peer counselors are accomplishing.

State and National Associations

Belonging to both your state and national association connects you with other people and other programs. Getting together to share information and ideas is very important in peer counseling, and both leaders and students find it beneficial. Students attending conferences with peer counselors from all different regions become aware their local group is not an isolated island but a part of a larger existing body.

In April of 1988, the fourth annual California Peer Counseling Association Conference was held in San Francisco with over 3,000 in attendance. For more information about the association and the annual conferences, you may write to the California Peer Counseling Association, 9300 East Imperial Highway, Downey, California, 90242.

The second National Peer Helpers Conference was held in Ft. Collins, Colorado in June of 1988. Leaders and students from across the United States spent three days attending workshops and gaining information and motivation. The address for the National Peer Helpers Association is 2370 Market Street, Room 120, San Francisco, California 94114.

The ABC's of Peer Counseling

I have found several key elements to a successful program. I call them the ABC's of peer counseling.

A—ACADEMIC: Make it an academic class, not a rap session.
ADMINISTRATIVE: Work with your administrators; try to have them claim some ownership for the program.

B—BEAUTIFUL: Fill the class with beautiful people from every group on campus. Remember all people become beautiful when they reflect the love of the class.
BOLD: Be bold in inviting important speakers to the class. Let them know what a special class they will be attending.

C—CONFIDENTIAL: Keep confidentiality.
CARING: Care about each student in class in such a way the student will model your attitude.

Rewards

The rewards to the teacher of the peer counseling class continue for years after the students have graduated. Seldom a week passes that I don't come in contact with a peer counseling alumni. We share a hug and greet one another as old friends. The bond created in class years ago continues.

Recently, I was in town and met one of the members of the very first peer counseling class on our campus.

"Mrs. Sturkie, I hear you are writing a book!" Kim exclaimed. "How is it coming?"

"Fine," I responded. "I have only a few pages to go, and it will be completed."

"Did you write about how I had helped Marshall his senior year?"

Seeing the puzzled look on my face, she continued, "You remember Marshall was having trouble passing some of his classes during his last semester; he was about ready to give up when I became his peer counselor. I worked with him, gave him encouragement, and he graduated."

"Yes, I do remember that now. I guess I had forgotten."

"Well, Marshall certainly hasn't. I run into him every once in a while; and just the other day, he told me again how glad he was that he'd graduated. He really is a super kid. I wish you'd told about him in your book."

"I will, Kim. I will."

Four years after graduation, Kim is still excited about a student she helped, and I am still being rewarded by peer counselors like Kim.

Epilogue

People who read this book have often asked me, "Do you still hear from the peer counselors whose stories appear in the book?" Or an equally common question is, "Wouldn't it be nice to know how these young people are doing now?" A more specific comment I hear is, "I'd really like to know whatever happened to Felicia—or Dave—or Mary—or Fran—or Tray—or Sue."

To answer the first question, "Yes, I do still hear from the peer counselors." And to the second question, "Yes, it would be nice for the readers to know how these young people are doing now." So, I contacted my friends and asked their permission to print some of their letters in the second edition of this book. Their real names again have been changed to the ones previously used for them. Other names they refer to, such as those of teachers, have also been changed to protect confidentiality. To all of you readers who have asked, "What happened to Felicia—or Mary—or Fran— or Tray—or Olga—or Dave—or Sue—or Kyle?" please continue reading. This chapter is for you.

From Sue — Chapter 2.

Dear Mrs. Sturkie,

Well, it has been a few years since I've last written to you. I believe when I wrote you last I had just gotten out of the drug and alcohol rehabilitation hospital. Today, I have three-and-a-half years of sobriety! Along the way some very wonderful things have happened in my life. I live a life of honesty, integrity, humility, and love. It hasn't been easy—I've had some challenging struggles. At times I felt as though I was trapped, unable to go back, and petrified with the thought of moving forward. But I have persevered! And I definitely have moved forward.

After leaving the hospital I lived in a women's recovery home for close to five months. It was one of the best things I have done for myself. My experience at the recovery home was full of love, growth, and friendship. Sort of like peer counseling! I also learned a bit of humility. I, the "princess" from a sheltered, upper-middle-class city, took on my first job as an elevator attendant. My transportation to and from work was by bus—in downtown Los Angeles! I wasn't then, but today I'm truly grateful for that time in my life.

I left the recovery home and became self-sufficient, financially and otherwise. I worked at a photo lab for some time and then braved going away to a university—depending solely on my own pocketbook. This proved to be a very challenging time in my sobriety. When I moved away to school (about two hours away from home), I isolated myself from friends, family, and the support group I had relied on. I felt extremely depressed and unhappy. I was on the edge of either going insane, going out and drinking again, or taking my own life. So, at the time, the most logical option to me was to withdraw from school and move back home. In retrospect, I do believe that was a very wise choice.

A little over two years have passed since my experience at the university. I have added to my adventure such things as working more, sharing an apartment with Mary, living through a semi-catastrophic event (an earthquake!), moving back home, starting school at the local community college, quitting work and going to school full-time, receiving exceptional grades, and feeling quite confident about myself and the direction I'm heading in life. I'm even assisting a good friend of mine in writing a book. You always said I'd be a writer—but my self-esteem was too low to believe you!

I've basically given you a very broad and boring outline of the last few years. Many events have happened to me. I've grown up a lot! But, I never forget where I began my journey of a wonderful, healthy, and sober life. It was in peer counseling where I received your unconditional support, where Mary came and shared her story, and where I learned very many valuable things. My friendships today are all the more tender and special because of peer counseling. In that class I not only learned about myself, my alcoholism and drug addiction, but I also learned how to reach out, hug, and be a friend.

Thanks you, Mrs. Sturkie ... for everything!

Love,
Sue

From Felicia — Chapter 3.

Dear Mrs. Sturkie,

It's difficult to believe that nearly six years have passed since the day I crossed the stage to receive my diploma. So much has changed in my life. I never thought I'd recover from what happened to me in my senior year, but here I am!

This Valentine's Day I was reminiscing about the changes in my life over the last few years, and I realized that you might like to be brought up to date.

Surprise— I made it to middle management! After trying college full time, I decided that I needed to experience a little bit of the real world. So, while I attend school at night, I have worked my way up the ranks and have a great job as the publicity and promotions manager at a local hospital. I love my work. It allows me to really express myself at the same time that I am helping the community. I never thought I'd feel this confident and assured of my professional future. I only have a few more classes to complete my B.A., and after I'm done with that— there's no stopping me!

If I know you as well as I think, you are reading this and wondering, "But how is she feeling?" Honestly, sometimes I really don't know. I know that I have worked through my feelings of guilt, betrayal, and even the anger. But I can't pretend that I am over the experience. I still get a hollow feeling when I think about what happened! I feel very sorry for a lonely, pathetic man (teacher) who could only gratify himself by stealing innocence. I hope he has straightened himself out and is functioning like a normal human being.

Recently, two years ago, I found a way to turn my anger into something productive. I guess I held things in too long. I was ready to explode. I sat back and examined my life. Why did I feel so self-conscious? Why did my relationships all fail so miserably (especially the physical part)? What was I doing punishing myself? Why did my dad leave? Why did I let men hurt, use, and abuse me?

I realized that the only person who controlled my destiny was me. Wow, I blew my own mind! So, I boarded a plane and flew to confront my enemy. Turns out, my enemy was a frightened, confused and lonely old man: my father. It was a cleansing experience. I really let him have it—maybe I overdid it, but I had so much anger built up inside of me that I exploded like a volcano. Surprisingly, he wasn't the lying creep that I remembered. He took his medicine and even admitted to his mistakes.

When I boarded that plane I felt as though a ten-pound weight had been lifted from my shoulders. For the first time in years, I felt as though I didn't have to hate or feel betrayed. It was all in *my* hands, and no one would control me like that again. I won't pretend that I answered all of my introspective questions on that trip, but I did answer the important ones.

Relationships still frighten me. I really believe that when I meet the "right" one this nagging expectation of betrayal will go away. I think I'm trapped in a tug-of-war between brutal reality and a Cinderella complex. Oh well, I've come this far—there's hope yet!

I've gone so far as to share some really personal stuff—like we used to in our "I feels" in peer counseling. I hope you are doing well! Please write. I'd love to help put a reunion together. That peer counseling class was full of some wonderful people. I truly miss our closeness, especially the "I feel" sessions.

How's Teddy? I understand you take him with you when you train others in peer counseling workshops. It gave me great joy to give him to our class. If he could only talk—what stories he could tell, and what love he could share. I hope, when you look at him, he reminds you of the tenderness and true love that he has to give. Hug him for me.

Love and friendship always,
Felicia

From Faye — Chapter 5.

Dear Mrs. Sturkie,

I have been going to our local community college for almost three years now. I've been doing well in all of my subjects except for mathematics and science, which were never my strong subjects, but I'm doing well. I'm particularly good in English, theater arts and humanities.

Personally, I have made particular strides in becoming more independent. I do things that perhaps a few months ago I wouldn't have thought I could do; for example, setting my own hair in hot rollers.

These things have made me feel more sure about myself; not that I wasn't sure before, but I feel better about facing my problems than I did previously. Also, the love and support I get from my parents helps me enormously. It's really a plus. Their enthusiasm over my future goals helps to accomplish what I set out to do. I plan to go away next year to a four-year college.

One of the major events that my family and I had was to go to Europe last summer. It was an experience that one must have in his or her lifetime. We visited England and France and had the time of our lives. It was everything that I dreamed it would be, only better.

With much love,
Faye

From Tray — Chapter 6

Dear Mrs. Sturkie,

Well first, Mrs. Sturkie, I hope you can read my writing because it's still just as bad as it was when you and I were in peer counseling together.

First a bit of the past. You remember I had peer counseling 1 and 2 with you when I was a freshman. After you left, I took peer counseling 3 and 4 with Shirley Goss and peer counseling 5-6 and 7-8 with John Coker. I had all four years of peer counseling and am very proud of it. For those last couple of years I carried a large case-load most of the time, but I always tried my best. Because of my experiences, I could understand what others were feeling with their situations.

Now out of high school (June '88), I work for a financial institution doing receptionist and gopher work. I am still a volunteer/cadet fireman with our city. I'm taking classes at night for my degree in Fire Science. I've been working in the fire service (part-time) for just about two years now and am very much on my way to being a fully trained and qualified firefighter/paramedic. Now, getting hired is the hard part.

I'm doing a lot better now than a couple of years ago. I'm not living with my mom and haven't been for about two years. We all get along much better, but we still have our moments. By the way, I'm living with my grandparents, and I'm blessed to have them.

Everyday I use the skills I learned in peer counseling. Everyday I encounter somebody who just needs to be heard and understood. My life now is so much more mature, full of knowledge and understanding of how people are on the inside, and how to love the person inside instead of the mask on the outside.

I am very thankful to God that He has blessed me with my family and friends like you, Mrs. Sturkie, and John Coker and all of the other special peer counseling people in this world. I am truly blessed with many gifts and many people who care and love me. Thank you, Mrs. Sturkie, you and peer counseling changed my life with your listening and love.

Love,
Tray

From Fran — Chapter 4

Dear Mrs. Sturkie,

I think of you so often, but seldom have time to write. It was 2 o'clock this morning when I crawled into bed, having just returned from work and picking up my daughter at my mom's. She'd been watching her while I was at work. I was very tired, but still had to set the alarm so I could get up early and get my child off to school on time.

I have my own apartment now and have really come a long way in the past five years, but it's been hard, damn hard. There have been days when I would have liked to have stopped being "Mommy" for just an hour—to have one hour of peace just to myself would have been pure heaven. But the thing about us moms is we are always on call. If you're a single mom it's harder because you have no one to share the daily responsibilities with. If you're a teenage, single mom it's even more difficult. If I were 30 or so, I'd probably have enough money for a baby-sitter on those difficult days, but we teenage moms don't have many luxuries.

There is no way I could have given my daughter a decent life or come this far without the help of my family. Up until just recently I have always lived with my family. Sure I would have liked the independence and privacy of living on my own earlier, but there was no money for that. I worked five days a week in the beginning. When I got my paycheck, after they took out for health insurance and I paid for daycare for my daughter, there was only enough left for gas and maybe a little extra. At that time my mom was working, and that was why there was a need for daycare during the afternoon.

My parents have paid for clothes, diapers, and baby food, and when (and if) my ex-husband paid any child support, I tried to pay them back and pay the pediatrician bills—no designer jeans or fancy cars for me.

Child support! What reaction that word brings. In the beginning I would get very angry when it was late. Sometimes it was even several months late. I couldn't help but think that Mindy's father had a major part in conceiving her and why, if he made a good salary, wasn't he contributing anything to her upbringing. I was the one who changed the diapers and cleaned the throw up out of the carpet. And it was I who would sit up in a steamy bathroom all night with her when she had the croup, or hold her all night because she had an earache or was teething and couldn't sleep. I did these things willingly even though I was so tired I could hardly function! This ex-husband of mine could never find someone to do what I do, nor would he have enough money to pay for it if he did. The least he could do is pay me the money he is supposed to for the care of *our* daughter. But I've learned now that being bitter and angry won't make it get here any sooner and if I depend on him he'll only upset me and let me down. I try to think of it as when it comes it's just like winning the lottery. It's something to hope for, but one can't depend on it. Oh, yes, this is the same charming man who said, "I love you and will always take care of you and the baby." Now he says the check is in the mail. The only contact he has with our daughter is on major holidays and big events.

After a while, my one job was not enough, so I had to work two. I'd take Mindy to nursery school in the morning, go to the first job, pick her up at five, leave her with my mom and work the second job. She didn't sleep through the night until she was about two-and-a-half, so I was completely exhausted during that time.

Eventually, I did start dating, but it wasn't easy. I worked five days a week and five nights a week, which included weekends. Needless to say, I worked seven days a week—to work only one job on a particular day felt like a day off. Quality time with my daughter was a half hour in the park, an occasional story before bedtime, or trying to calm a temper tantrum when I was already late for work.

When Mindy was about three-and-a-half, I had a steady boyfriend. I can remember getting home from work, trying to change my clothes, cooking a fabulous dinner, and cleaning the house (in a frenzy) before he got there. I did all of this only to hear him complain later in the evening when my daughter would not easily go to sleep after being put in bed. I'm sure she felt like she was missing out on something, and just wanted to spend some time with me because I was gone so much. Instead of my boyfriend trying to go out of his way to be involved with Mindy and bond with her, he would judge my parenting skills. He considered Mindy a nuisance, not an asset. Because he had never been a parent he thought he knew all the answers. Being a parent you never know all the answers. You just have to rely on instinct, love, and your own upbringing and hope you are doing the right things.

My pregnancy did affect my whole family. It was certainly not something they anticipated for me, and like myself, they had different dreams for my young adulthood. It meant my sister giving up being the youngest. Up until that time she was the cutest—not only did she have to share that spot, but she also had to make sacrifices, as well as help by babysitting. I was very lucky to have my family to live with and depend on, though sometimes it was difficult. I was a mother, but living with my family, I was also a child, and I had to follow rules and do as I was told.

My relationship with my boyfriend ended a year later when my dad was transferred out of state. Because I was unable to afford both childcare and rent, I had to move. I had hoped very much that my boyfriend would ask me to marry him, but he was not ready for that commitment. My daughter and I are a package deal, and it takes a rare individual to be able to fall in love with not just a person, but a family. It was very difficult for me to lose him, and even after I moved, I tried to hang on. He came to visit me, but the closer we got, the farther we grew apart because it scared him when things were going well. He didn't want the responsibilities of an instant family.

When my parents moved, I ended up moving in with other family members. While in transit I was visiting my relatives and got a very good job offer. My parents, my support network, were a full day's drive away. It was extremely hard for me. I lost my friends, my boyfriend, and my parents—but I needed to work and at the time it was the best opportunity I had. Several months later while visiting my folks, I got an unexpected job offer and grabbed it. My parents helped me get an apartment, and because they take care of my daughter while I'm at work I'm able to pay rent.

I really feel good about where I'm at now, but its been a long climb. If you are wondering if I still feel like I made the right decision—I believe I made the very best decision for me—the only decision I could live with and feel good about. Every time my daughter gives me a hug I know that all the sacrifices and difficulties were worthwhile. She is a very healthy, bright, and beautiful child—very outgoing and loving. I'm very lucky to have her, and I'm lucky to have a family that has made it possible for me to raise her.

My family provided me with a car, a home, and tremendous emotional support throughout these years. Without their help I would have had to go on welfare. There were many problems during the time of my divorce over custody and visitation. My getting pregnant and having my daughter did not only affect my life drastically, it involved every member of my family. I was very lucky that they were willing and loving and made sacrifices for me.

Love,
Fran

From Kyle — Chapter 7

Dear Mrs. Sturkie,

You are to me as a rose in spring
A reminder of how sweet life can be.

In 1985, I left our city and went away to college. When I arrived, I found there were no support groups on campus except for those specifically related to addiction. So, part out of my desperate need to be listened to, and the fact others desperately needed to be heard also, I lead a group where listening carefully to each other was the main theme. Mostly we gathered in a circle and did "I feels". Some facilitation, encouragement, and eliciting questioning was done. I went to the college psychologist for consultation. He was very little help, since he was only one person for a 300-student campus. In time the support group dwindled.

Then a friend began a co-counseling support group class, similar in theory to peer counseling though much more advanced. Recognizing that active listening is most important in counseling, co-counseling also recognized that almost every person has been hurt in ways which render us unable to easily release stored up feelings. We need special attention to help us get into and through those feelings. Co-counseling offered a wide range of tools as well as a palpable model of what human beings are like.

So I dove in and began practicing and bonding with others in the support group. I also joined a men's group, active in the city near my college—not a college men's group. I went to a workshop on loving limitlessly, and one on classism (how being from a particular monetary class relates to the hurts and confusion we receive from the society).

Then I returned to Los Angeles and began co-counseling regularly with three other men. This lasted for almost a year—hard work, bonding and consistency. I led a campaign to get a man elected to the local school board—he was 20 years old, qualified, and would have given a voice to the youth in the schools.

In the spring of '88, I took a job at a hospital. I worked with youth and adults with chemical addictions and/or psychiatric problems. It was challenging to say the least.

Then I went on a youth expedition primarily to experience a "developing" nation. I also wanted to reconnect with people my age and to give myself the opportunity to lead young people. I had not felt generally at ease with people my age since junior high. It was very hard—perhaps it prepared me for the next step, which was to be a big one as well.

Now I live in Santa Cruz. I moved here in August '88. There was a large co-counseling community here, and I dove right in. I thought about the living situation I needed, so I put an ad out for a healthy household where warmth, sharing, playfulness, openness, encouragement and support were the foundation.

I joined a co-counseling support group, began counseling regularly, and going after what I really wanted in life in Santa Cruz: health, sports, play, being physical and living in nature (the country is full of life up here—the forests, streams and ocean.). I built, as well as found, my way into the large community. Dancing, on and on and on.

Soon I will be going back home for a visit. I hope to gather old friends whom I felt separated from back in junior high. I want to reconnect and repair that old separation—to share what is "good about being a man" and "what is not." Also to share what's happened for the last many years.

Recently, I noticed that I felt separated, disconnected, from young people—high school age and junior high—so I reached out to a young woman who is leading her own constituency (young people—young women) and offered her my attention on whatever she wanted. Step by step I'm reconnecting with all kinds of people and taking on more challenging and enjoyable endeavors.

I love you,
Kyle

From Olga — Chapter 4

Dear Mrs. Sturkie,

I have so much to tell you, I hardly know where to start! First of all, I can wish you happy New Year, since today is the last day of 1988. I hope the new year will bring much happiness and success to you!

Many changes will take place for me which I welcome warmly. I hope that most of my plans will turn out well, and if they do, I will move to Los Angeles in August. I hope to get a trainee position at a Norwegian travel agency. I have been in touch with the Norway Trade Council in Los Angeles who have been very kind and so far helpful! They have promised to do as much as they can to help me get a job—and I hope they will. Perhaps the major reason of this arrangement is to see how well James (yes, the same James that I met and started dating when I was an exchange student) and I will function in a day to day relationship. We really care an awful lot for each other, and we both feel a lot of pain being apart. But I do need working experience for the department I want to join at the University here in Norway. It's a requirement; the students have to be able to relate the literature to real working life. Since it doesn't matter how or where I get my work experience, I might as well get it in Los Angeles living near James. In theory I have everything planned—but please, keep your fingers crossed it will actually turn out my way!

Hopefully, James will come to Norway in June. We will see as much of Norway as we can, introduce him to my family and friends, and then we are off. James will finish his engineering education at UCLA, and I will work. I feel very excited and happy about our plans, yet I know there are many pieces which have to be placed before I can be sure. I guess I leave some to destiny, but since I'm a very practical person I'm doing as much as I can to prepare!

My sister who is a journalist is now working at a news television station. It's very nice to see my last name on television. She is very talented and is doing a good job.

Thank you for your postcard from your trip. How was it? Did my fellow Europeans treat you and your family well? Did the bookfair in Frankfurt bring good things for your book? I'd enjoy a long letter telling me all about it.

I hope you had a nice Christmas with your family and a good rest too!

With much love,
Olga

From Mary — Chapter 2.

Dear Mrs. Sturkie,

I now have five years of sobriety! How neat it would be to sit in our peer counseling class once again, and share my success with all the friends who supported me from the very beginning.

Remember how I met Sue—when I returned to the peer counseling class to speak. Well, not only did peer counseling put Sue and me together in a time of need for her, but it gave me a great roommate. Both Sue and I had always lived at home, and we decided to move out on our own about the same time. So we found an apartment big enough for the two of us and became roommates. It worked out perfectly. We both worked and attended the community college.

For about three years, I worked in the field of alcohol and drug recovery while attending school. Then I made the decision to go to school full time, and moved over two hundred miles away from home. It has really been a challenge. I had always had my mom and dad for support, and living this far away without them or my friends has been difficult at times. But I have experienced real growth.

Remember the boyfriend I had for the past four years? I had to let him go.

He could not maintain his sobriety. Needless to say, breaking up with someone who meant a lot to me was very difficult, but knowing what to expect in the grieving process has helped me let him go. And God has replaced him with two fabulous friends.

The next time I visit Mom and Dad, I'll give you a call. How about us going to that little Mexican restaurant for lunch?

Love,
Mary

From Dave, Chapter 11

Dear Mrs. Sturkie,

Remember, I was a freshman in high school when you taught my peer counseling class. Now I am a freshman at a small liberal arts college. Much has happened in the past three years, but I will try to keep this letter short.

First of all, let me start out by saying that although my life and the life of my family has gone on, and we seem to be doing pretty well, there are times when the pain of a sudden realization hits me, and I remember the pain of my parents' divorce. The holidays are still difficult, especially for my mom, but each year it gets a little easier. There always seems to be something which comes up that reminds me my family is not what I consider to be ideal. This year we have just recently sold our house, the house I grew up in. I saw it as the final symbol of my parents' divorce. That house holds a lot of memories, good and bad, some of which are hard to let go of.

Anyway, let me tell you about some of the really great things that have happened to me. I think it was about the time of my sophomore year that things really started moving for me in my life at school. I got very involved in theater and music and had wonderful experiences in plays and musicals and in choirs. I met many good friends through my involvement and gained a lot of confidence and support from them. During my senior year in high school, I got up the confidence and ambition to take on the job of a member of the student council. There, too, I met wonderful people who showed me by their example what it means to be a leader, a success, a good person. So overall, I had a good high school experience.

I can honestly say that peer counseling helped me to get everything that I did out of school. It taught me how to go through a crisis and come out intact. It also taught me how to experience the joy of sharing with other people. I am still a person who keeps things inside, but peer counseling gave me some way of expressing my feelings honestly. It taught me also to try to help other people understand their feelings through the simple act of listening.

Best wishes to you, Mrs. Sturkie.

Yours truly,
Dave

From the current peer counseling teacher at Brownsboro High school.

Dear Joan,

Lately, I've been feeling a need to write and give you an update on the status of the high school peer counseling program which you created seven years ago. On the surface, the program seems to be simply part of the curriculum, but as was the case when you were here, the real impact is with the emotional support the program provides for students.

The successes are sometimes difficult to see, and when they appear it is dramatic. Not that it will surprise you, but the depth of pain we find young people having is surfacing almost on a daily bases. Since the peer counseling classes meet daily, students reveal *heavy* issues often. We are pushing the concept of being open so much that we have coined a slogan: "The healing is in the revealing, not in the concealing."

Joan, I would like to share with you two of the more involved cases which represent the value of having a peer counseling program. First, I call this case, the lost child. George Parker, an English teacher, came to me about four years ago and indicated his concern about a student who seemed very lonely. The student, Ray Burke, was a freshman; and as we observed, he never seemed to be with anyone. His clothes were dirty and generally unkept. I assigned one of our peer counselors to talk with Ray to determine if our concerns had merit. After the first meeting, it was obvious this kid needed support. The peer counselor worked with Ray for the rest of the year. What a turn-around. Ray began wearing clean clothes and walking up-straight; his grades and social skills improved dramatically. This story is an example of how peer counselors can, and do, make a difference.

The second case I want to tell you about involves suicide. Wow! Does this strike fear into me every time it appears. You may remember Warren Davis — the bright, good-looking, talented player on the water polo team. He killed himself two years after his high school graduation. Where are the support groups when students leave high school? Peer counseling and sports provided Warren with the love of a family while he was here, but after graduation there was nothing. Warren wrote a letter to the captain of his high school water polo team giving everything he owned to him. He laid out his three year books from high school on his bed, opened to the water polo team pictures. Then he drove to the beach, went for a swim, came back to his car, climbed into the back seat and shot himself to death. How we need to provide programs like peer counseling at all levels of our society. Since Warren's death we have worked extra hard here at the high school on preventing suicide. But we live in a very fragile society.

This year alone, we are working with three students who have attempted suicide. Betty, Julie, and Nancy either took pills or cut their wrists. Of course, we have them seeing a professional counselor, but the effect on the peer counseling program has been revealing. These suicide attempts have scarred peer counselors. We have brought in experts to work with the students in establishing support groups. Now many of the peer counselors feel more comfortable with the issue of suicide. But they remain alert, as I do, whenever a peer seems depressed.

Well, I could go on but it's time to close. I don't know what or how things would have turned out if we didn't have peer counseling. Thank you for your genius and hard work in starting our program. I believe we have saved many young people as a result.

Love,
John Coker

Bibliography

Adler, Ronald, and Neil Towne. *Looking Out/ Looking In.* New York: Holt, Rinehart and Winston, 1981.

Alberti, Robert E., and Michael L. Emmons. *Stand Up, Speak Out, Talk Back.* New York: Pocket Books, 1970.

Berkovitz, Irving H., and Jerome S. Seliger. *Expanding Mental Health Interventions In Schools.* Volume One. Dubuque, Iowa: Kendall/Hunt, 1985.

Bower, Sharon, and Gordon Bower. *Asserting Yourself.* Reading, Mass.: Addison-Wesley, 1976.

Brammer, Lawrence. *The Helping Relationship: Process and Skills.* Englewood Cliffs, N.J.: Prentice-Hall, 1973.

Carkhuff, Robert R. *The Art of Helping VI.* Amherst, Mass.: Human Resource Development Press, Inc., 1987.

D'Andrea, Vincent, and Peter Salovey. *Peer Counseling Skills and Perspectives.* Palo Alto, Calif.: Science and Behavior Books, 1983.

Egan, Gerald. *You and Me: The Skills of Communicating and Relating To Others.* Monterey, California: Brooks/Cole Publishing Co., 1977.

Egan, Gerald. *The Skilled Helper,* 3rd Edition. Monterey, California: Brooks/Cole, 1986.

Furstenberg, F., Jr., J. Menken, and R. Lincoln. *Teenage Sexuality, Pregnancy, and Childbearing.* Philadelphia: University of Pennsylvania Press, 1981.

Gray, H. D., and J. Tindall. *Peer Counseling: In-depth Look at Training Peer Helpers.* Muncie, IN: Accelerated Development, 1985.

Harris, Thomas A. *I'm O. K. - You're O,K.*, New York, New York: Avon Books, 1967.

Hebeisen, Ardyth. *Peer Program for Youth.* Minneapolis, Minn.: Augsbury Publishing House, 1973.

Hendricks, Gay, and Russel Wills. *The Centering Book.* Englewood Cliffs, New Jersey: Prentice-Hall, 1975.

Johnson, David. *Reaching Out.* Englewood Cliffs, New Jersey: Prentice-Hall, 1972.

Johnston, L. D., J.G. Bachman, and P.M. O'Malley. *Highlights from Student Drug Use in America 1975-1981.* U. S. Department of Health and Human Services, Public Health Service, National Institute on Drug Abuse, 1982.

Kar, Snehendu B., John Talbot, and Carl Coan. "Peers as Health Promoters Among Adolescents," Education for Health, Issue No.1, 1986.

Kennedy, Eugene. *Crisis Counseling—The Essential Guide for Nonprofessional Counselors.* New York: Continuum Publishing Company, 1986.

Kubler-Ross, Elisabeth. *On Death and Dying.* New York: MacMillan Publishing Co., 1969.

Loughary, W. John, and Theresa M. Ripley. *Helping Others Help Themselves.* New York: McGraw-Hill, 1979.

MacFarlane, Kee, and Jill Waterman, with Shawn Conerly, Linda Damon, Michael Durfee, and Suzanne Long. *Sexual Abuse of Young Children.* New York: Guilford Publications, Inc., 1986.

Moustakas, Clark E. *Loneliness.* Englewood Cliffs, New Jersey: Prentice-Hall, 1961.

Myrick, Robert D., and Robert P. Bowman. *Becoming a Friendly Helper: A Handbook for Student Facilitators.* Minneapolis, Minnesota: Educational Media Corporation, 1981.

Myrick, Robert D., and Tom Ervey. *Caring and Sharing.* Minneapolis, Minnesota: Educational Media Corporation, 1984.

Myrick, Robert D., and Tom Ervey. *Youth Helping Youth.* Minneapolis, Minnesota: Educational Media Corporation, 1985.

Myrick, Robert D., and Don L. Sorenson. *Peer Helping: A Practical Guide.* Minneapolis, Minnesota: Educational Media Corporation, 1988.

Peck, M. L. *Youth Suicide.* New York: Springer Publishers, 1985.

Rogers, Carl R. *On Becoming A Person.* Boston, Mass.: Houghtin-Mifflin Co., 1961.

Samuels, Mimi and Don. *The Complete Handbook of Peer Counseling.* Miami, Florida: Fiesta Publishing Corp., Educational Books Division, 1975.

Satir, Virginia. *Self Esteem.* Milbrae, Calif.: Celestial Arts, 1975.

Sturkie, Joan, and Gordon R. Bear. *Christian Peer Counselors: Love In Action.* Dallas, Texas: Word Books, 1989.

Van Cleave, Stephen, Walter Bryd, and Kathy Revell. *Counseling for Substance Abuse and Addiction.* Waco, Texas: Word Books, 1987.

Van Ornum, William, and John B. Mordock. *Crisis Counseling With Children and Adolescents—A Guide for Nonprofessional Counselors.* New York: Continuum Publishing Company, 1983.

Varenhorst, Barbara. *Real Friends.* San Francisco: Harper and Row, 1983.

Varenhorst, Barbara, with Lee Sparks. *Training Teenagers for Peer Ministry.* Loveland, CO.: Group Books, 1988.

Wallerstein, J.S., and J. B. Kelly. *Surviving the Breakup: How Children and Parents Cope with Divorce.* New York: Basic Books, 1980.